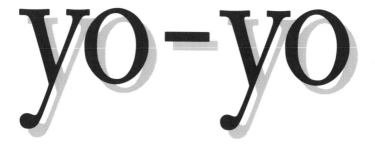

yo-yo

Relationships

How to Break the
"I Need a Man" Habit
and Find Stability

DOREEN VIRTUE, PH.D.

DEACONESS PRESS
Minneapolis, Minnesota

Published by Deaconess Press, 2450 Riverside Avenue South, Minneapolis, MN 55454

Library of Congress Cataloging-in-Publication Data
Virtue, Doreen, 1958-
    Yo-yo relationships : how to break the "I need a man" habit and find stability
    by Doreen L. Virtue.
    p. cm.
    ISBN 0-925190-35-7 : $12.95
    1. Women--Psychology.   2. Man--Woman relationships.
    3. Interpersonal relations.   I. Title.
HQ1206.V57   1994
155.3'33--dc20   94-21345
                                                                        CIP

First printing: October 1994

Printed in the United States of America
97 96 95 94 93   7 6 5 4 3 2 1

Cover design by The Nancekivell Group
Interior design by Designsmith

Publisher's Note: Deaconess Press publishes books and other materials related to the sub-jects of physical health, mental health, and chemical dependency. Its publications, includ-ing *Yo-Yo Relationships*, do not necessarily reflect the philosophy of Fairview Hospital and Healthcare Services or their treatment programs.

TO MY BROTHER,

KEN HANNAN,

WITH LOVE, APPRECIATION AND ADMIRATION.

CONTENTS

PART FOUR—TAKING CHARGE
GETTING MORE STABILITY IN YOUR WORK LIFE

ACKNOWLEDGEMENTS

This book was made possible by the talented and innovative team at Deaconess Press. I especially want to thank Jay Johnson, who had many heartfelt discussions with me during this book's development. Jay really understood the premise of this book, and his enthusiasm was enormously appreciated.

Thank you, too, to Ed Wedman and Jack Caravela for your belief in this project. I also want to say a heartfelt thank-you to Carla Waldemar for her support, patience and superb editing. Also, thanks to Jay Hanson for layout and production help. And a big thank-you to Bob Morris, who worked with me during my first book's publication and is working with me once again! I love when life comes full circle, don't you?

I also appreciate the incredible people I'm fortunate enough to have as friends and family. Thank you for your ideas, brainstorming, input and support, Bill Hannan, Joan Hannan, Michael Tienhaara, Charles Schenk, Grant Schenk, Linda Izzo, Joel Scheinbaum, M.D., Helene C. Parker, Ph.D., Melinda White, Silvia Aslan, Heide Miller, Brian and Barbara Tracy, Dr. Susan Jeffers, Jan Hannan, Caryn Hannan, Candice Hannan and Caitlin Hannan.

PREFACE

Do you ever feel something is missing from your life? Does your mind play the "if only" song over and over. The song is "If only I had a (better husband, better boyfriend, more money, better job, different car, different house different apartment, better figure, college degree, etc.), then life would be better?"

Do you ever feel your life is a roller coaster—a rocking ship on a stormy sea—a yo-yo? Perhaps, like other women, you're sick of constant turmoil and problems, and you crave stability and calm. You wonder what conditions you could change to achieve the peace you so desperately desire. If only your marriage, love life, career, education, weight or family were different, then . . . .

The only trouble is—and perhaps you've already discovered this—even after your wishes are met, you still feel the same way! Something still seems to be missing. It's very frustrating to work and work on achieving a goal and remain unsatisfied and unhappy. We feel frustrated, ripped off, betrayed because we believed our hard work would be rewarded with feelings of serenity and security.

As a psychotherapist, I've worked for over a decade with women grappling with this issue. This book doesn't judge our natural tendency to look for happiness outside ourselves. Instead, it offers alternative methods for tapping into true sources for happiness, pleasure and fulfillment.

When we look for fulfillment through people, places and things, we give away a lot of control over our lives. Our lives "yo-yo"—fluctuate through terrifying and exhilarating ups and downs—because these other people, places and things are "yo-yo-ing." We, in essence, have tied ourselves to the strings of their yo-yos, and then are flipped along like the end car of a roller-coaster.

Taking control of your life means getting your wishes met without letting go of responsibilities. The methods described in this book aren't based on theories; they're based on hard data, derived from my many years of working with women all across the country.

You'll discover why I firmly believe that fun is a necessity, not a luxury. Unless we actively add fun to our lives, our health, finances and relationships suffer. When you begin to understand how important fun is to a successful career and family, you won't feel guilty for taking pleasure for yourself. And the best part is that the extra energy you get from adding fun to your life helps you get more things done in less time. *You'll feel you've got an extra two or three hours in the day!*

You'll also read about embracing life and diving into it head-first. Too many women postpone their dreams, waiting for someone to tap them on the shoulder and say, "It's time! Start your goals now." But no one is going to give us permission. It's also true that our relationships with our children, coworkers, spouse and family improve when we feel better about ourselves.

Today, women face enormous pressures like never before. We have to balance work and family, look great, be a super hostess and make lots of money! The pressures can feel overwhelming. I've addressed realistic remedies for escaping the stress and guilt associated with juggling so many roles.

My wish for you is that you'll take advantage of the wonderful solutions available to you RIGHT NOW. You *can* balance career and family and still have time for exercise and fun. In fact, you *must*. Your life and your happiness depend on learning how to enjoy and embrace this balancing act. You deserve happiness, and you can give it to yourself starting now.

—*Doreen Virtue, Ph.D., Newport Beach, California*

Something Is

Missing from My Life

CHAPTER ONE

Welcome to
the Jungle

Susan, a bright, accomplished woman in her early forties, was in my office for psychotherapy because she was unhappy and didn't know why. "I can't put my finger on it, but something's missing," she told me. "I have a pretty good marriage, a nice house, great kids and I love my job. I should be happy, but I just don't feel it."

Another client, Mindy, also complained of a vague unhappiness. "I feel like my husband should be making more money," Mindy said with evident resentment. "We live in this dumpy little house and we really need a new car. If he'd get off his butt at work, he could make a lot more money and we'd be much happier." Mindy felt disappointed—almost betrayed—by her husband's lack of earning power.

Still another client, Barbara, voiced dissatisfaction from a different source. "I know what would make me happy," she told me. "If I could only lose thirty pounds, then my husband would be romantic, like he was in the beginning. Then our relationship would improve, and I'd feel better about myself. I have so many goals I want to accomplish, like getting back to painting and finishing my college degree. But I feel so bad about everything, I have no energy to start on projects!"

Fortunately, Susan, Mindy and Barbara learned that taking care of oneself is not "selfish," but actually a gift to everyone. They used the methods outlined in this book to tap into their inner source of happiness and zeal for life.

Let me explain what I mean when I say "being good to yourself is actually a gift to everyone" by asking if you remember how you felt when you'd see your mother frowning, hard at work vacuuming or cleaning. Did you feel a little scared of making her mad—maybe guilty—because she was cleaning up your mess? How did the sight of your tense, unhappy mother make you feel?

Compare that feeling to how you felt when you saw your mother relaxed and smiling, enjoying herself and laughing. Didn't that feel safe, warm and good?

You have that same impact on your own children, spouse, family and friends. When you are happy, you have a tremendously positive effect on them. So it's not selfish to make yourself happy. It's a gift to everyone who loves you.

Welcome to the Jungle

My workshops and talk-show appearances have taken me across the country, giving me opportunities for heart-to-heart discussions with many women. I invite these conversations wherever I can—in airports, on planes, at restaurants, at workshops, on talk shows. And everywhere I go, I hear a collective voice of frustration.

We learned in the 1980s about the Superwoman Syndrome—so now we have a name for what we continue to do in the 1990s. Actually, I've observed that women are doing even more in the '90s than we were in the '80s. Here's a slightly tongue-in-cheek picture of a '90s Woman's typical day:

The Modern-Day Super Hero

The alarm screams. She can't believe it's time to get up already! Did she really sleep last night? No time to complain about being tired, though—there's so much to do!

Get the kids' breakfast! Next, frantically make sure they're ready for school. Her husband wants to know where his red striped tie is. "What? Do I look like a computer or something?" She's instantly sorry for snapping at him. After all, her life's got enough friction.

"Where are those pantyhose I just bought?" her frazzled thoughts scream as she rummages through her dresser. She rearranges the tear in an old pair so it's hidden inside her shoe.

Next, an outfit: What to wear, what to wear? One of these days, she promises herself she'll get more organized. She'll lay out her clothes at night and jump into them in the morning. Okay. For now, though, she pulls that reliable blue suit off the hanger and stuffs her hips into the too-tight skirt. She's already worn the blouse once; it really should be at the dry cleaners, but there's no time to think about that now! A little extra cologne under the arms and no one will know the difference.

The clock nags at her incessantly: "You've got a meeting in one hour, and it takes forty-five minutes to get to work—if you're lucky and there's no traffic! Sally loves it when you're late to meetings so she can make herself look good to the boss. And you've been late to the last three meetings. Tsk, tsk, tsk."

"Shut up, clock!" she screams in her mind.

She rounds up the kids, prods the youngest into the car, and blows a kiss to her husband as she screeches out of the driveway. Damn it, she forgot her briefcase!

"Oh come on—the car's out of gas already? Didn't I just fill the tank last week? Oh well, there should be enough to get the kids to school and me to work. Besides, I don't have time to stop for gas—and even less time if I run out."

She tries not to think about it.

Okay, five more minutes and she'll be at the office. The meeting starts in ten minutes, so that will be perfect. So why is her heart racing, why is she perspiring?

"Parking spot, parking spot, come on, come on. Run to the meeting. No time to grab coffee, damn it. Brush your hair with your fingers, and don't think about your overwhelming need to urinate. Deep breath, then open the door. See Sally look at her watch as you enter, without breaking stride in her conversation with the boss."

The rest of her day is just as frantic and stressful. She lives on coffee and diet cola, and on good days she squeezes in aerobics class on her way home. And every night, she manages to coordinate dinner for the family.

The dishes are washed at her harried insistence. As the family flops in front of the television, she straightens the living room. A phone call from work with questions about the big project she's working on. A knot in her stomach as Sally's name enters the conversation.

Her husband flips through the mail and hands her the bills, since she's the family bookkeeper. "We need more money," she thinks. "I need that promotion—not Sally."

A Victoria's Secret catalogue rests in her husbands hands; he points to a model in a peach demi-bra and thong bikini. "That would be a great outfit on you," he smiles. "Yeah, right," she shoots back before she can stop the sarcasm. "That's all I need," she thinks. "Not only do I have to take care of everyone, handle office politics, be sweet and make money. Now I have to look like a lingerie model, too!"

Welcome to the jungle.

We Know Better, But at What Price?

Women are still new to the world of competition. Boys have lived with it for years, through sports teams and cowboy-and-Indian movies. We little girls were content playing Barbie-and-Ken-get-married games. Everything was cooperation. If any girl in the neighborhood acted snippy or out of line, a neighborhood mom straightened her out. In a worst-case scenario, little girls would ostracize any little prima donna until she submitted.

The 1980s whetted our appetites for fine dining, pretty cars, pretty houses and power suits with short skirts. We had a small taste of paychecks and power, and we were hooked. Many of us promised our bank officers we'd continue making money to pay off mortgages and credit cards.

We tried to do it all, and they called us Superwomen. Super Mom, Super Businesswoman, Super Aerobics Queen. We were tired all the time but didn't know why.

After a thousand self-help books, *Cosmopolitan* articles and Oprah episodes, we now know what we're doing. We know we're overdoing it, trying to be perfect in too many areas of our lives. But we can't quit yet. The competition is too stiff, because there's always some woman out there who might take our job or our husband away from us.

We are just now learning how to handle competition without letting it kill us–a lesson that men have learned through their lives. But can't we have more? Can't we learn to successfully manage our responsibilities and still enjoy the simple joys and pleasures? Or is "having it all" just a dangerous myth? Not if you take charge of your life and learn to rely on yourself—not some man in your life—to get it for you.

In the next few chapters, you'll read about creative solutions that have worked for other women. Read on, and you're likely to find a solution that fits your needs, too.

CHAPTER TWO

Taking Charge: A Balancing Act

Thirty-eight year old Theresa, who owns a printing business, attended one of my workshops centering on balancing work, family and fun time. It was 8:30 on a weeknight, and she'd been working hard all day.

To get to know the audience, I asked questions about stressors in their lives. First, I asked the audience members to raise their hands if anyone owned a business. Theresa raised her hand.

"Anyone live with another adult?" Again Theresa's hand went up.

"How about having a teenager at home?" A handful of audience members' hands shot in the air, including Theresa's.

I continued my questions, asking, "How many:
- of you have children under the age of 13?"
- commute more than 30 minutes a day to or from work?"
- are experiencing financial difficulties?"
- are taking care of an elderly relative?"
- are attending night school?"
- are involved in team sports?"

Theresa raised her hand in response to every question. I explained that each question pertained to common stressors that compete for attention with our free, personal time. These stressors can rob us of enjoyment and energy unless we take measures to add fun and pleasure to our lives.

Every day we are bombarded by responsibilities and commitments–things we must do out of moral or financial obligation. We choose how to divide our day's hours to meet these commitments, and if there's time left over for us, that's when we relax and have fun.

It's just like paying our bills, isn't it? We get paid, and then slowly hand out increments to the mortgage company, landlord, grocery store, finance company and utilities. If there's anything left, we may splurge on something for ourselves.

I'm going to suggest reshuffling this arrangement more in your own favor. In the end, you'll have more time, money and enjoyment out of this new "economy."

A Snapshot of Your Life

This quiz is the same one I've used with groups throughout the country for the past ten years. Thousands of people have taken this test, and I've studied their answers while researching ways to balance work, family and personal needs. The test provides important, accurate information if you answer it candidly, without regard for what you think your answer "should" be.

Most people find the answer that first enters their mind is the most honest and accurate. Take a moment, then, to answer this test to get a picture of what your life's balancing act looks like right now.

TRUE or FALSE   T   F

1. I have friends with whom I can talk whenever I'm feeling upset or need help.

2. Most of the time, I feel that other people accept me for who I am.

3. I'm very happy with the way my life is structured right now.

4. My interactions with my family are usually pleasant or satisfying.

5. I feel like I have enough free time for hobbies or relaxation.

6. I have fun and laugh and play on a regular basis.

7. I feel loved by my family and friends.

8. I receive personal fulfillment, security or peace of mind from my spiritual/religious life.

9. Most mornings, I wake up feeling refreshed and rested.

10. I feel good, in general, about the shape my body is in.

11. I usually have no problem falling asleep and sleeping soundly through the night.

12. I exercise three or more times every week.

13. My health is usually good; I rarely get sick with colds, the flu or other ailments.

                                                    T   *F*

14. I enjoy physical activities, like dancing and sports.

15. My sex life is enjoyable and satisfying to me.

16. I *don't* depend on colas, coffee, tea, candy or cigarettes to boost my energy level.

17. Most days, I look forward to going to work.

18. I enjoy learning new things.

19. I usually feel like I'm in charge of how my time is scheduled.

20. I often read books or articles about topics that are new to me.

21. I've noticed that as I grow older, I'll sometimes change my opinions about important issues.

22. If I really believe in a cause, I'm apt to take a stand for it, even if it means risking ridicule.

23. I like meeting new people and hearing about their careers, travels and other experiences.

24. I have set clear goals, both short-term and long-term, for myself, and I'm actively working toward them.

Scoring

There are no right or wrong answers on this test, only accurate or inaccurate answers. The test scores aren't like points on an aptitude test. They're more like a gauge showing your "intended priorities" and "actual priorities."

Add the total of true answers for questions one through eight, and write your total here:

Section One_____

Next, add the total true answers for questions nine through sixteen, and write your total here:

Section Two_____

Finally, add the total true answers for questions seventeen through twenty-four, and write the total here:

Section Three_____

Interpreting Your Scores

This self-test looks at three parts of your life: your emotional, physical and intellectual components. By scoring this test, you'll see how much of your time, attention and energy you're currently investing in these different parts of yourself.

SECTION ONE: Your Emotional Life

Zero to Three True Answers: Warning

You are dangerously low on "emotional fuel." You may be experiencing depression, including blue spells or crying. Scores below three in Section 1 mean you are not putting time into your emotional side, such as having fun, maintaining friendships or forming deep relationships. You may feel too busy, pressured or isolated to put time into yourself, and guilt may be a factor in keeping you from fulfilling yourself.

Four to Six True Answers: "A" for Effort!

You are probably feeling okay about your personal life, but may find it's a constant tug-of-war with other responsibilities. You struggle to find time for play, friends, church and family. Sometimes, playing feels like a job!

Seven to Eight True Answers: Congratulations!

You have put a lot of thought and energy into taking good care of yourself. Probably, you learned the hard way that emotional nourishment is a necessary part of taking care of yourself and the people you care about.

SECTION TWO: Your Physical Life

Zero to Three True Answers: Sedentary, but Not Happy about It

Most people taking this survey score low in Section Two. That is because, when it comes to deciding how to spend time, exercise and physical upkeep are last on the list. In a 1993 survey by the President's Council on Physical Fitness, 64 percent of Americans said they didn't have enough time to exercise. Chapters in Part Three of this book discuss realistic ways to incorporate exercise into your life. Other important areas in Part Three include getting enough sleep and having a healthy diet.

Four to Six True Answers: Health-Conscious

You have a fitness program started, or firmly in place. You're not one hundred percent happy with your figure, but then, who is? You're working on improving your body, and it shows. Although it's sometimes a struggle to find time for exercise, you manage to work out at least three times a week.

Seven to Eight True Answers: Fitness Buff!

If you answered true to seven or eight questions in Section Two, you are very rare indeed. Very few women feel this good about their health and bodies, so you are exceptional. Even pro athletes have nagging feelings of doubt about their looks and fitness levels. So, if you are this confident about your body, you've done something right. If nothing else, your lack of guilt is a healthy sign!

SECTION THREE: Your Intellectual and Career Life

Zero to Three True Answers: Burnout and Stagnation

Are you bored with your job, feeling stuck or unchallenged? Maybe it's time to enroll in that night school class and finish your degree. Are you in a rut due to retirement or unemployment? How about learning a new subject or skill, either through reading, talking to someone new, or taking a class?

Four to Six True Answers: Balanced

This is a good sign, signaling you are sufficiently energized by your career or educational pursuits. You look for interesting challenges, such as asking friends about their trips to Europe or signing up for that Saturday class on French cooking or business law.

Seven to Eight True Answer: Stimulated, but Are You Happy?

People who score high in Section Three usually are happy with their lives and turned on by their careers. Sometimes, however, high scores in this area signal workaholism. Are you putting all your energy and attention into work and the pursuit of money at the expense of personal relationships and fun time? Have you let your body go—possibly endangering your health— while you climb the corporate ladder? The only one way to interpret high scores in this area is by completing the next section, Overall Scoring.

Overall Scoring

Now look at the three scores in Sections One, Two, or Three. A balanced life means having three section scores that are roughly the same: for example, five, six, and five. If your scores vary more than three points from one another, this shows a life out of balance. Most people taking this test (over 5,000 people to date) score four or five in Section One; two or three in Section Two; and five or six in Section Three.

Fun Belongs in Your Life

In discussions in my workshops, I hear lots of complaints from people who don't have enough time for fun or exercise. Their responsibilities to family and work are enormous and can't be ignored.

These women literally work seven days a week, from the time they get up until the time they go to bed. In further chapters, you'll read the protests they gave me for why they couldn't put fun in their lives. Then you'll read how they overcame this resistance and guilt about having fun.

These busy women remind me of the man on the old variety shows who would spin plates on a stick. Remember him? He'd spin a plate on one stick, then another and then another. He had to keep the first plate spinning, or it would fall on the floor shattered into pieces. This man had to attend to seven or eight plates simultaneously!

Have you ever felt like that plate spinner, ferociously attending to simultaneous emergencies? How are you supposed to remove your attention from the "plates" long enough to have fun without experiencing disaster?

Many of the plates in real life spin better on their own. Many plates spin longer and faster if you're happy and relaxed. And how can you relax in the midst of chaos? With heavy doses of fun.

Families enjoy and cooperate more with a mom who's confident and assured rather than a woman who is harried and on edge. Men gravitate to women who know how to enjoy themselves. Company crises are resolved by a cool head. And solutions for tight finances are the product of a fertile, creative mind. You fuel creativity, confidence and charisma by having fun. Seriously!

Is fun a goal of yours? Would you like to have fun—and be successful in work, love and fitness? The good news is that these areas are not mutually exclusive. Actually, the opposite is true. If you learn to incorporate fun into your life, you will make more money, have better and more stable relationships and have time for exercise and better health. Sound too good to be true? It is true, as you'll read.

The rest of the book is divided into three parts, each corresponding to Sections One, Two, and Three of the questionnaire. Each section is important, and if you answered three or fewer "trues" in any section, you may want to concentrate on that section in the following chapters.

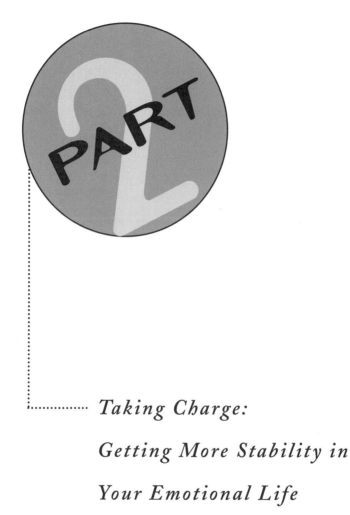

PART 2

Taking Charge:

Getting More Stability in

Your Emotional Life

ABOUT PART TWO: YOUR EMOTIONAL LIFE

In Part Two of this book, we'll examine different areas of our emotional life. The main emphasis of Part Two is on building strong love relationships, and this is no accident. As women, we place tremendous importance on love, romance and family.

I recently conducted a formal written survey of one hundred-fifty women, who were not in therapy and who considered themselves "happy with their lives." I asked them what factors contributed to this happiness.

In the survey, I listed things that normally make us happy, as you can see in the list below. From this list, each woman chose the factor that most contributed to her happiness and the factor second most important to happiness.

The following page contains the list and directions as they appeared on the survey. How would you respond to this list?

Please write a 1 next to the item you consider MOST important to your happiness. Then write a 2 next to the item you consider the SECOND MOST important to obtaining happiness.

Children_____   Job Satisfaction_____

Health/Diet/Exercise_____   Spirituality/Religion_____

Money_____   Good Spouse/Lover_____

Education _____   High Self-Esteem_____

Friends_____   Nice House, Car, Etc._____

Attractive Figure _____   Travel/Leisure Time_____

Other

(Please specify)_____

Other

(Please specify)_____

The majority rated High Self-Esteem as the most important ingredient in happiness. The second-most important ingredient—and this surprised me—was a Good Spouse/Lover. Children was the third-most frequently chosen important ingredient.

When looking at answers to "What is the second-most important contributor to happiness?" most respondents answered Good Spouse/Lover. In fact, when you combine the total responses for what these women perceive as the most important and the second most important factors leading to happiness, Good Spouse/Lover was the top answer!

I also asked the women two other questions that yielded interesting results:

What is the biggest factor influencing your happiness or unhappiness with your life right now?

What, if anything, do you feel is missing from your life right now?

What do you think were the top answers to these two questions? Right! Relationships, Love and Marriage were the most frequently given responses. These women, who all have successful careers, rated Relationships and Love as the most important influence on their happiness and unhappiness, *above all other factors!*

Why Are Relationships So Important to Us?

Sometimes I think we women are obsessed with relationships. We are so absorbed with analyzing our man's behavior and thinking about ways to get his attention and love. If we put this same energy into our careers or education, we would never feel financially insecure again!

This obsession with having a perfect relationship creates the Yo-Yo Relationship Syndrome. We keep the relationship under a microscope and analyze it to the point of becoming depressed, anxious or even physically ill. We complain about his bad habits and selfishness to our best friend, a process that reinforces our negative beliefs about the relationship. Crying on your best friend's shoulder isn't therapeutic or cathartic; instead, it erodes the foundation of the relationship until it eventually crumbles like a decayed building. Then we break up or divorce and feel momentarily relieved—until we realize: Oh no! I'm alone without a man!

The Ups and Downs of the Yo-Yo Relationship

This is the Yo-Yo Relationship Syndrome. We bob up and down on a string, feeling out of control. Our minds snap back and forth, telling ourselves one moment, "I've had it with relationships! I don't want to be with a man for a while," and the next moment thinking, "But what if I wait too long and miss out on my true love? After all, I'm not getting any younger." We convince ourselves, "What I really want is a nice rich man to spoil me," only to decide, "The only relationship worth having is one built on the solid ground of shared values and love." Down, up, this way, that way, propelled by forces outside ourselves. It's enough to make you want to become a nun!

To break out of the Yo-Yo Relationship Syndrome once and for all, we have to put into action all those principles we already know deep inside ourselves. Let's face it: We are smart women who overcome adversity every day. We handle business affairs, juggle family and community responsibilities and even manage to keep the car running smoothly. We can put those same smarts into action to take charge of our emotional life.

In Part Two, we'll focus on three key points essential to taking charge of your emotional life:

1. Adding Fun to Your Life

This is the most important point of this book. If you don't have fun regularly, you won't feel in control of your life. Fun is a basic human need. As you'll learn in the chapters to follow, if this need is unsatisfied, our effectiveness and power is obstructed in every facet of our life.

2. Choosing the Men in Your Life Wisely

The usual way the Yo-Yo Relationship Syndrome is triggered is by getting involved with the wrong guy. Just like choosing healthful ingredients at the grocery store to make a healthful meal, there are ways to select a healthy man to make a healthy relationship. There's no need to waste months or years in discovering he's really an inappropriate guy for you!

3. Tips for Avoiding Unnecessary Relationship Problems

Both men and women unintentionally create arguments and misunderstandings because they don't understand fundamental "do's and don'ts" of gender differences. Since this is a book for women, the chapters all focus on ways to avoid unnecessary misunderstandings with your boyfriend or husband. There are certain trigger words and behaviors that men interpret differently from women.

Sometimes, we need to confront and argue with the men in our lives. But most of the time, we just want peace and harmony. There are ways to maintain and control this peace in your love life, and the chapters in Part Two gives lots of insights into these ways to keep your relationships stable, calm and smooth.

When your emotional life is running smoothly, you'll have more time and energy to devote to your career and physical fitness. And as both your finances and body get stronger and healthier, there's less need to feel dependent on a man for security and strength. This self-reliance helps us to detach and stop obsessing about the relationship. And when we stop worrying and fretting about the relationship, it has room to grow. Couples can focus on their strengths and united goals instead of spending all their time discussing problems. The yo-yo has been put to rest.

Sound good? Then, let's continue?

CHAPTER THREE

Fun Is a Necessity, Not a Luxury

"When I Relax I Feel Guilty"

I can't emphasize enough the importance of taking time to enjoy yourself every day. The next chapter lists suggestions for incorporating fun into your life without experiencing guilt or disaster (two fears that keep us from enjoying ourselves!).

I think the majority of people, especially women, are suffering from Fun Deprivation. Like an anorexic who shuns food, we turn away from anything smacking of relaxation or pleasure.

Here are some of the underlying beliefs that keep us from enjoying ourselves. See if you recognize any of your own thoughts or beliefs about fun:

"If it's fun, it isn't valuable."

"If it's something I want, I can't have it or don't deserve it."

"I can't relax until I make more money."

"If I let down my guard, someone else will get ahead of me."

"If I relax, others will think I'm lazy."

"If I ask for what I *really* want, others will think I'm selfish."

"I'm valued and prized most when I'm being productive."

"Fun is frivolous and a waste of time."

"I'll have fun next week … month … year."

"Getting ahead in life means constantly keeping your nose to the grindstone."

"Only bums relax."

"To me, work is fun."

"I feel guilty when I'm not working or doing something productive."

"The only justification for taking a day off of work is illness, a snowstorm or a death in the family."

How Fun Deprivation Spoils Love Relationships

Many of the women I've worked with have legitimate concerns that keep them from enjoying themselves and their relationships. They feel pushed for time. "If I take a moment to relax and have fun, I'll never get anything done!" they tell me.

In Chapter Four, you'll learn some methods for incorporating fun into your life and how—in the long run—enjoyment and pleasure will give you extra energy. You'll feel like you've got an extra two or three hours in each day, because your joy and enthusiasm (fueled by fun) allows you to embrace new challenges instead of letting them defeat you.

Here are the stories of three of my clients who felt they had no time for fun. They came to me for help when their relationships began to dissolve and disintegrate. We worked on the underlying fears and beliefs that pushed them to work instead of play. Sometimes, a fear of intimacy or fear of losing control caused the drive to overwork. Other times, a lack of energy (caused by a fun deficit!) made tasks take twice as long to get done.

Patricia, a single mother of two young girls, had an intensely demanding schedule. She juggled her job as marketing director with caring for her children. She was also completing her MBA degree, which meant long evenings in the classroom and long weekends spent studying. Patricia's plate was very full.

After Patricia had been dating Mark for nine months, he began protesting about the amount of time Patricia devoted to activities outside their relationship. "You're always busy!" he complained. "I only get to see you once a week, and that's not enough."

She had no idea how to please Mark and still fulfill all her other obligations and responsibilities. Patricia enjoyed Mark's company, and she genuinely valued their relationship, but how was she supposed to make more time for him?

Andrea's situation was a little different. The owner of a small boutique, Andrea spent long hours working alone in her store. Her only human contact was with customers, and Andrea interacted with her customers in a very businesslike, no-nonsense way. Her only source of close, warm, human connections was through her husband, Timothy.

When Andrea would see Timothy in the evening, she'd engulf him with her emotional neediness. She'd demand his undivided attention and felt upset if Timothy so much as read the mail while she was talking. Her need for "friendship" was insatiable; Timothy encouraged Andrea to seek friendships through women's groups or church activities. But Andrea protested that she had no free time to spend outside work and home.

Unlike Patricia and Andrea, Charlene didn't work outside the home. But she sure did work inside the home! Charlene was intent on keeping her small three-bedroom house perfectly tidy and dust-free, despite having two toddlers and a husband living there.

She spent a lot of time chasing her children's messes and picking up after her husband (a chain-smoking beer drinker). Charlene was perpetually frustrated, as her family seemingly worked against her goals. "They're impossible," Charlene told me. "No matter how much I scream, bitch or complain, my kids and husband just throw their stuff wherever they want. They know I'll pick up after them."

Charlene and her husband argued constantly. She said he was a slob, and he countered that she was much too serious and a compulsive housecleaner.

She was actually avoiding emotional intimacy with her family by throwing herself into her housework. Charlene had underlying beliefs that made her feel guilty if she relaxed. Her beliefs were, "I'm only valuable if I'm producing" and "my house is a reflection of my worth as a human being."

Every Human Being Needs Contact and Emotional Support

Next to the death penalty, the worst punishment for prisoners is solitary confinement. Without human contact, people suffer and imagine they're going crazy.

Studies show that babies raised without human contact and nurturing also suffer tremendously. Their learning rate is blunted, and their emotional maturity may be affected as well. Research shows every living organism requires contact and nurturance. Infants crave the touch of their mothers or a mother-substitute.

If you scored three or fewer true answers in Section 1 of the quiz in Chapter Two, you are likely to be suffering from emotional deprivation. Like the infant away from his mother's arms and the prisoner locked in a solitary cell, your heart hungers for laughter and love.

You know something's wrong or something's missing, and you may try to fill the gaps with outer-focused activities—work, shopping, eating, gambling or love affairs. But the missing ingredient isn't outside, it's right there inside of us. Just like Dorothy in *The Wizard of Oz* who found she'd had the power to go home all along, so do we have the power to create stability and satisfaction.

In Sections Three and Four, you'll read how "fun deprivation" interferes with our physical and intellectual, or career, lives. Exercise programs that aren't fun are abandoned. If we are unfulfilled emotionally, we act differently at work. We become needy and may even appear "weak" to others (which is dangerous around "shark types" at the office). Emotional neediness makes us crave attention and appreciation from the boss. The boss, of course, is preoccupied with his own job and doesn't have the time to focus on fulfilling our emotional needs.

That's why it's so important to fill up those emotional needs— especially having fun, relaxation and pleasure—before and after work. We must take responsibility for getting our emotional needs met. We must take charge of our weekends and schedule in some "down time." Guilt-free time!

CHAPTER FOUR

You'll Get More Done, If You First Have Fun

We get so caught up in being productive that we resist and fear having fun. When I ask women in my therapy practice or at workshops to think of one fun thing they could do before they go to bed that night, I often meet with blank stares. You'd think I was asking them to name the capital of a remote country or to solve a calculus problem!

Why is my request to "have fun" met with this reaction? After talking to many women, I've heard several patterns in their answers.

1. "I Need to Devote My Energy to My Children and Husband."

There's nothing wrong with being devoted to the family, of course. But too many women hide behind the apron skirts of "family responsibilities" instead of venturing out to have fun. Sometimes, underlying fears ("If I'm not a perfect wife and mother, my husband will leave me.") punctuate this behavior.

2. "First I Have to Accomplish My Goals, Then I'll Have Fun."

The surprising irony of this reason is that it is backward! Yet, this is probably the most common complaint I've heard from women. Plans for fun are put on the back burner, pending that elusive day when the MBA is completed, the job promotion attained, and the house decorating is finished.

Here's the good news: If you schedule in one daily dose of pure fun, you'll feel more joy and enthusiasm. These positive emotions fill you with energy that will spur you to accomplish more goals than you ever dreamed possible!

3. "I Can't Be Selfish!"

When I hear this phrase, I always ask for a definition of the word "selfish." *Selfish* is an odd word. There definitely are dimensions of selfishness that should be avoided, such as being thoughtless, manipulative or antisocial. But putting fun into your life is no more "selfish" than performing other necessary functions, such as eating, drinking and sleeping. You can't live without these vital ingredients!

4. "Other Women May Need to Have Fun, but I'm Above All That!"

This belief is a product of the Superwoman Syndrome that says, "I'm strong and I'm special. I don't have ordinary needs, and I can overcome anything." This belief pushes women to work overtime at their jobs and homes, ignoring exhaustion and proving how resilient they are.

The Only Fun That Counts Is Pure *Fun*

Here's how I define fun:

Any activity where the only goal is pleasure. Period.

Children naturally have pure fun—just for the thrill, pleasure,and joy. What did you do for fun as a child? When did you feel happiest? If you can't remember, then you might spend some time watching children play. Notice how they revel—without a sign of embarrassment, reluctance or guilt—in the pure joy of touching the sky with their feet as they swing, or coaxing a kite higher and higher. Remember when you used to do stuff like that? You haven't outgrown your appetite for fun any more than you've lost the need to eat and breathe. If anything, we need to laugh *more* now that we're responsibility-laden adults!

Activities with other goals attached to them, like winning, scoring the most points, making money and so forth, don't meet this definition of fun. They might be pleasurable activities, but they are not "pure" forms of fun.

Competitive activities such as golf, bowling, tennis or racquetball are pleasurable, but they don't count as "pure fun." The competitive dimension counteracts the pleasurable dimension. Likewise, if you're self-conscious and compare yourself to others, activities that lend themselves to self-consciousness—country-western dancing, skiing and surfboarding—do not qualify as "pure fun." And if you count "going to amusement parks with my kids" as a fun activity in your life, let me ask if you really enjoy yourself on these outings. Can you let go and have a blast? Or are you frantically herding the children to long lines waiting to get on the rides, wondering how to relieve the pain in your feet?

Of course, I'm not suggesting abandoning golfing, bowling, family outings or skiing. These activities definitely have their value in our lives. But, just like we need to eat a well-balanced diet, a well-balanced life has healthy doses of pure fun on a regular basis.

Mix the competitive or self-conscious pleasures in with the pure fun activities and balance with meaningful work, healthy love and family relationships, and voilà: You've got a stable, satisfying life!

Here's How to Add Two to Three More Hours to Your Day

Of course, I don't mean to sound as if I'm oversimplifying my prescription for a balanced life. I realize how valuable each and every minute of the day is to you, and how difficult it is to squeeze one more activity into a crammed-jammed schedule! You might even be thinking right now, "So now I'm supposed to add fun into my life, on top of all my other responsibilities!" I know, I know, it's the equivalent of asking you to spend your last dollar on a get-rich-quick plan.

But I do want to ask you to try this experiment for one week: if you do one fun activity every day, you will have more energy every day. Judge the results yourself. You will feel as if you have added two to three more productive hours to your day, because:

- You will get your work finished in less time, because you won't be slowed down by heavy feelings of frustration, burnout and resentment.
- You won't get into as many time-consuming arguments with your children, spouse or coworkers, because you'll be in a better mood and won't get baited into frivolous bickering.
- Other people will be attracted to your light-heartedness, and they will be more apt to help you.
- Your energy level won't have the highs and lows that lead to erratic productivity. You will wake up more excited about the day and find yourself feeling energized until bedtime.
- You will think more clearly and be able to quickly and creatively solve problems.

Keeping Promises to Yourself to Have Fun

When I first became a therapist, I worked in an alcohol and drug abuse rehabilitation hospital. Ninety percent of my clients were men. I became used to dealing with the little uncertainties of working with alcoholic male clients. For example, if they had an appointment to see me at 3:00, they would show up at 3:10.

Then I left the alcohol and drug abuse treatment center to open my unit for people with eating disorders. The demographics of my client case load changed dramatically. I was no longer treating men who were high on drugs. Now I was working with women. Successful, powerful women who felt in control of everything in their lives, except for their weight and overeating.

When these women had an appointment to see me at, say, 3:00, they'd arrive at for the appointment at 2:55! These women, these Superwomen, are incredibly punctual and a joy to have as a therapy client.

There's a common denominator that explains why they are overweight, as well as why they are always on time: A Superwoman is perfect at keeping promises to others, and lousy at keeping promises to herself.

Instead of fighting, judging or analyzing this tendency, I choose to capitalize on it. If you know this about yourself—that you keep promises to your husband or boyfriend, mother, best friend and committee chairwoman, but rarely carry through on promises to yourself to diet, eat right, exercise, and so on—then why not use this tendency to your advantage?

One Hundred-One Ideas for Adding Fun into Your Life

At my workshops, I ask audience members to promise the person sitting next to them, "I am going to do one fun thing for myself before I go to bed tomorrow. And that fun thing is (fill in the blank)." Sometimes I ask group members to exchange phone numbers and call one another to check up on their "assignments." This really works, and the workshop attendees know I'm right. They know that unless they promise someone else, they'll never get around to having fun. I call this a Fun Promissory Agreement.

In my therapy practice, I've had to assign clients to go and have fun. I've given other clients discounts on therapy sessions in exchange for their doing one fun thing every day. There's so much resistance to having fun that I have to bribe my clients! Unless they promise someone else—me, their friend, their daytimer schedule book—that they will have fun, it never happens.

So, here, I'm going to ask you to do the same thing. Promise someone (me and this book, if you need to) that, before you go to bed tomorrow, you will engage in one fun thing for yourself.

The two major symptoms of "fun deprivation" are:

1. Feeling tired, cranky and irritable and that your life is out of whack.

2. Forgetting what "fun" means.

I always ask the women in my workshop to give me examples of the fun things they do. Here's some of their answers, taken from actual transcripts of my workshops:

- "I'm going home from work early tomorrow." ("That's great!" I thought, before hearing the rest of her plans for "fun.") "Then I'm going home to sew my daughter's school uniform."

- "I'm going to the dentist, because I think taking care of yourself is fun." (It's true that taking care of your body keeps your self-esteem high—but would you call going to the dentist pure fun?)

- "I'm going to aerobics class." (Again, I believe there's confusion between the concepts of "taking good care of oneself" and "having fun." They are two distinctly different needs, like sleeping and breathing, and both are important. But, again, like sleeping and breathing, the two needs are dependent on one another, but not interchangeable).

Here are some suggestions for fun things to do. Some of these ideas may fit your idea of a "good time," while others may not. Everyone, of course, has different tastes, temperaments and budgets—all factors influencing what kind of fun best suits you.

It's a good idea to stretch yourself a bit, though, and try something new. You might be surprised how much fun it is, for example, to attend a basketball game and cheer for the home team. Fun comes from unexpected sources, too. You might derive intense pleasure from volunteering time at a local convalescent center and forming a special relationship with one of the residents.

If you're really adventurous, you could try every item on this list, one by one! Just think what pleasure you'll experience as you "work" your way through this fun-filled list:

1. Go to a comedy club.

2. Get a full-body massage.

3. See a funny movie.

4. Take a bubble bath, and don't forget your rubber duckie.

5. Flirt shamelessly with the next man you see.

6. Test-drive the most exotic sports car you can find.

7. Organize a slumber party for your female friends.

8. Read the comic page in the newspaper before reading anything else.

9. Buy yourself something that's not on sale.

10. Get real dressed up, like Ginger Rogers, and go ballroom dancing.

11. Get boudoir photos taken of yourself (no matter what your shape, these specialty photos will make you feel like a dazzling centerfold!).

12. Rent a boat at the local lake and take it out for a picnic on the water.

13. Have a Cappuccino at a popular restaurant and indulge in people-watching.

14. Make up the stupidest joke you can possibly think of.

15. Call your best friend from high school.

16. Rent a convertible car for the day and take it for a long drive on an isolated country road.

17. Get a group of friends together for Sunday brunch.

18. Ask the next person you talk with to tell you a joke.

19. Throw a chocolate-dessert and champagne potluck get-together.

20. Go to the most expensive dress shop in town and try on a couple of outfits that you'd love to own.

21. Paint your fingernails and lips a shameless shade of red.

22. Ask your husband or boyfriend for a backrub, and don't return the favor right away (because that undoes all your relaxation).

23. Change your hairstyle or hair color, or add highlights to your hair.

24. Rent a limousine for the evening and have a "Cinderella" night on the town.

25. Plant flowers that are already in bloom.

26. Buy a new pet.

27. Go on a one-day backpacking excursion and explore the local mountains.

28. Sign up for creative arts classes, like photography, gourmet cooking or stained-glass making.

29. Close the drapes, turn on the answering machine, and read the trashiest novel you can find.

30. Invite your closest friends over to watch *Sunset Boulevard.*

31. Pop some popcorn and experiment with different ways to prepare it (with caramel, cheese, salad dressing, chocolate syrup, etc.).

32. Go to a bar with your husband or boyfriend and pretend to be strangers picking up on one another.

33. Gaze at the clouds and identify animals and other familiar shapes.

34. Pack a lunch with bread, cheese and wine, put on a flowing white dress and have an old-fashioned, romantic picnic with your man or best friend.

35. Go to the local convalescent hospital and read stories or letters to an elderly person—positively heart-warming!

36. Take a special friend to a nightclub frequented by people slightly younger than you. Pretend you're ten years younger than you really are, and dance the night away!

37. Go to a karaoke bar and sing your favorite song in front of everybody.

38. Buy a scratch-off lottery ticket, but don't scratch it just yet. Instead, dream about all the ways you'd spend the money if you won.

39. Buy a feather boa and wear it around the house just to be silly and sexy.

40. Go to a crafts store and buy silk flowers to make a pretty floral arrangement.

41. See a play at a local college or small theater.

42. Have a sing-along around the piano with your family.

43. Go skinny-dipping.

44. Play a board game with some friends.

45. Call a local talent agent and see if he'll represent you as a "real-person" actress, model or voice-over talent (you never know!).

46. On a hot summer day, make a "slip and slide" out of heavy plastic tarps and water from a hose.

47. Call a group of friends and go bowling without regard for who "wins" or "loses".

48. Rent a horse at the local stable.

49. Go to the local pool and make yourself dive off the high board—thrilling!

50. Fill up water balloons on a hot day and throw them at each other.

51. Visit a travel agent and get vacation brochures to fuel a "mental vacation".

52. Write yourself a love letter.

53. Page through your old photo albums.

54. Play strip-poker with your boyfriend or husband.

55. Housesit for someone, and get a real change of scenery.

56. Play your old favorite song, and ask your husband or boyfriend for a dance.

57. Borrow someone's dog and take it for a long walk.

58. Join a softball game.

59. Go to an amusement park and ride the tallest roller coaster.

60. Have a pillow fight with someone.

61. Slather whipped cream or pudding on your husband and on yourself!

62. Spend the evening at a local hotel and order dinner from room service.

63. Look for "casting call" ads in the paper, and audition for a part as an "extra".

64. Take turns babysitting for your neighbors, so you all have the opportunity to have kid-free evenings.

65. Spend the weekend at a bed-and-breakfast establishment.

66. Load your camera with film and take nature pictures.

67. Gather wildflowers for a breathtaking bouquet.

68. Dress up in a disguise and see if anyone recognizes you.

69. Just for today, forget your diet and have that double-chocolate piece of cake.

70. Go to the park and play on the swings and slides.

71. Take the day off from work and see a matinee movie.

72. Get a pedicure, complete with a long foot rub.

73. Put a Do Not Disturb sign on the bathroom door and take a really long bubble bath.

74. Fly a kite.

75. Get a triple-scoop ice cream cone.

76. Go for a long bicycle ride.

77. Take a physical exercise class that's out of the ordinary: karate, ballet or water sports are good examples.

78. Have a facial.

79. Put your feet up on the coffee table and watch a "brainless" show.

80. Go to garage sales and consignment shops and collect bargains.

81. Organize a neighborhood potluck get-together.

82. Start that novel you've always dreamed about writing.

83. Go to a new restaurant and order something completely different from what you normally eat.

84. Take the day off and resolve to do nothing but relax .

85. Go to a local club and listen to a jazz or blues band.

86. Put together a beautiful aquarium, complete with exotic fish and decorations.

87. Buy a new cassette tape or CD for your stereo.

88. Bake chocolate chip cookies and eat the dough.

89. Call the local radio station and request it to play your favorite song .

90. Attend a ball game, wearing a hat or shirt with your favorite team's logo, and then jump up and loudly cheer every time your team scores.

91. Go fishing.

92. Splurge on a vacation to an exotic locale (a weekend in San Francisco, perhaps?).

93. Go to a bingo game.

94. Go snorkeling at a barrier reef.

95. Chase your husband or boyfriend around the room, then wrestle on the floor and tickle one another.

96. Ride a merry-go-round.

97. Shop for an outrageously funky Halloween costume (even if it's months away) at second-hand shops.

98. For one whole day, use a phony accent and pretend you're from a different country.

99. Send anonymous "You're Great!" cards to all your friends, and sign them "Guess Who?"

100. Climb into bed and devour that book you've been meaning to finish.

101. Buy and use the most fragrant soap and complementary lotion you can find—the scent will put you in a lighthearted mood!

CHAPTER FIVE

Declare Your Freedom from Guilt and Worry

In my psychotherapy practice, I've spent more time on two needless roadblocks to happiness than any others: guilt and worry. I refer to these emotions as "needless" because, too often, a person suffers under the weight of negative thoughts and feelings but doesn't take action to remedy the source of the emotional pain. To me, guilt and worry are calls to action! If something is bugging you, you must take care of it.

In this chapter, we'll examine clinically proven methods for curbing guilt and worry before they have a chance to drain your energy and zest for life. We'll also discuss other time-wasting emotions, such as bitterness, resentment, jealousy and frustration. And finally, because women have been raised to squelch anger, we'll look at healthy ways to express and release anger.

"Is It My Fault?": The Heavy Burden of Guilt

I've worked with many parents who feel guilty about their children. Among the common statements I hear are:

- "If only I hadn't divorced my husband, then my daughter would have gone to college and had a better life."
- "If only I had spent more time with my children when they were young, maybe they wouldn't be in trouble now."
- "If only I hadn't had my son when I was so young, then maybe I would have been a better mother. I was too young to be a parent and wasn't prepared to accept all the responsibilities."

I've heard countless other guilt-laden confessions having to do with all sorts of circumstances. I've listened to thousands of heartfelt regrets that weigh heavily on the souls of women who are already overly burdened with responsibilities and problems.

Whenever I hear one of these guilt-based proclamations, I ask my client the same question: "What can you do *now* to rectify or correct the situation?" Because, to me, *the only value to guilt is using its energy to better your life or the world around you.* If you wallow helplessly in guilt, nobody wins. Ruminating about "what I should have done" will attack your spirit and body—and may very well shorten your life. Then your children really will have an absent mother!

Guilt Is Not the Same As Shame

Guilt and shame are often used interchangeably, yet they are quite different terms. Bestselling author and counselor John Bradshaw once told me a clear-cut definition of the difference between guilt and shame. He said, "Guilt is feeling bad about an act you did or didn't perform. Shame is feeling bad about who you are as a person."

As a psychotherapist, I've seen this distinction in action. Women who were abused as children are particularly prone to feelings of shame for who they are as persons. Sexual-abuse survivors often carry feelings of inferiority or being damaged into adulthood. Adult children of alcoholics often feel inferior to others, after years of hearing emotionally abusive messages from their drunken parents such as, "You're a no-good kid!"

Feelings of being inferior or damaged often require psychotherapy to uncover and heal.

The most difficult part about asking for, and accepting, help is that women who feel ashamed of themselves often are hanging onto a thin shred of self-esteem. They fear that asking for therapy will validate their feelings of being damaged, and that what little dignity and self respect they have will be shattered. How happy they are later when they discover that therapy doesn't remove their last remaining bits of dignity. Instead, therapy pumps up their self-esteem to levels they never dreamed possible. They enter therapy feeling weak and afraid, and they leave therapy feeling renewed and strong!

It is not a sign of weakness, instability or insanity to seek a therapist's assistance in rewriting your self-image. I've had many clients, who first entered therapy as senior citizens, tell me, "I wish I'd gotten therapy when I was a lot younger, because I wasted a lot of years feeling bad about myself." These women had believed they'd outgrow early childhood feelings of being a bad or inferior person—or that they deserved them. But such feelings usually don't change without outside intervention, such as therapy.

Attack Guilt at Its Root

Guilt, if left untreated, eats away at our physical and mental health. Guilt is the acid that dissolves our zest and enthusiasm for life. It makes us sour and creates self-fulfilling negative prophesies. When we feel guilty, we don't like ourselves as much as we could. Other people sense our low self-esteem and naturally are repelled by it. So we feel rejected by others, when it is our own doing!

The only way to get rid of guilt is to take action. Here are some of the ways my clients successfully evicted guilt, the unwanted houseguest in their souls.

Forgive Yourself

If you regret something you did in the past, remind yourself that you were doing the best you could at that time. Ask yourself: "If your best friend had done what you did, would you forgive her?" Often we hold much higher standards for ourselves than we do for those around us.

Make Amends, If You Can

The 12-step programs have taught the value of apologizing for past misdeeds, whenever possible. If saying "I'm sorry" is a difficult prospect for you, then consider writing your feelings on paper and mailing your apology.

Resolve Never to Repeat the Mistake

Easier said than done, true. But often the pain of guilt is great enough to prevent us from making the same gaffe twice.

Use Your Hard-Won Wisdom to Help Others

All humans are prone to the same types of earthly foibles you now feel guilty about. So it stands to reason that you could help others from making the same mistakes as you. Some of our greatest biographies, fables and self-help books are written by people who "have been there." The same goes for recovering drug addicts who share their battle stories in free speeches to young people to encourage them to say no to drugs. In this way, our suffering has new meaning, and wasn't a waste of the preciously few moments we are allotted in life.

Worry Not, My Love

My dear paternal grandmother spends much of her time worrying. She worries about people she loves getting sick or hurt. She worries that people will steal her possessions or that natural disasters will occur. She calls my father or my uncle for reassurance, and, as loving sons, they willingly listen and reassure her with calming words.

I think it's a shame that at this stage in her life, Grandma is unable to let go, relax and simply enjoy all the gifts in her life. After all, she has a great personality and sense of humor, and people (especially men!) adore her. She's still a gorgeous woman, with some of the prettiest legs I've ever seen! She's an interesting person, well-read and well-traveled. And she's financially secure and surrounded by loving relatives and friends in one of the prettiest cities in America.

Yet Grandma's worrying is a mental habit she developed many years earlier. As with most habits, it's difficult to identify and to change.

Do you worry needlessly? In other words, do you spend time worrying, when you might otherwise be enjoying yourself? Like guilt, worry is only needless when it doesn't result in a corrective action.

Here are some techniques that psychotherapists and researchers recommend for overcoming the worry habit. You might find that one or two of these methods is especially effective in instantly easing worrisome thoughts and feelings:

The Worry Time Technique
This method, devised by bestselling psychologist Dr. Wayne Dyer, involves setting aside a scheduled hour for worrying. During the day, when a worrisome thought arises, write it down and tell yourself you will worry about it during your appointed Worry

Time. For example, say you're worried about being able to afford a present for your boyfriend's birthday. Write that thought down.

By writing the thought, you instantly reduce your worry level because you won't worry about forgetting what is important to you. A big part of the thought pattern we call "worrying" is a circular style of recirculating a thought around and around in our minds. We are worried we might forget something important. If you write the thought down, you won't worry so much about forgetting to do or accomplish something.

Then, if your scheduled worry time is between—for example— 6:00 and 7:00 p.m., you take out all your written-down worries, and during that hour you concentrate on nothing but what is worrying you. During that hour, focus on your worries and give them your undivided attention.

Dr. Dyer's technique may sound slightly tongue-in-cheek, but it does have valuable results. If you really keep your promise to yourself and consistently engage in a worry time, you will find your mental worry habits changing for the better. You will be able to remove worries from your mind because you will trust yourself to take care of the worry later.

Also, by concentrating on worries during a regularly scheduled, uninterrupted time, you are more likely to achieve concrete, creative solutions to the problems. You're likely to find more resolve to conquer the seemingly unconquerable problems in your life. When you think of solutions, be sure to write those down next to the "worry" on your paper. Then put a little check mark or the word "Resolved!" next to each worry as you conquer it.

Affirmations

Sometimes it's the little nagging voices from the past that spoil the present moments in our lives. Old voices from our childhood might pop up unexpectedly in our minds, saying cruel things like, "You're going to fail and make a big fool of yourself." Then we worry, because we erroneously believe these old voices are prophesies of impending doom.

Therapists, such as I, spend a lot of time helping clients erase these needless old tapes of the past. Sometimes the negative messages from the past are difficult to identify because they are such an ingrained part of our belief system. Maybe we heard our parents criticize us for so long that it's now second nature for us to criticize ourselves. Or perhaps one of our professors warned us that we would always be a "no-good loser," or some other equally damning fate.

If you turn on the lights in an insect-ridden house, you'll see cockroaches scramble to return to the darkness. The quickest way to scare out those old negative thoughts is to "turn the light on" them. The best way I know to do this is through affirmations.

Quite simply, affirmations are the polar opposite of negative thoughts. They are sentences that affirm goodness. Pay close attention to your thoughts as you read the following affirmations. If you have a lot of leftover negative beliefs, they will make themselves readily apparent as you read this list of positive beliefs. As the negative beliefs pop up, you can "catch them and trap them" in a mental "roach motel" by writing them down as they become apparent. Then, keep reading these affirmations over and over, every day, until you no longer hear any accompanying negative thoughts. At that point, you'll know you have trapped and destroyed all those nasty creatures that previously caused you to worry!

I deserve good.
I am a successful person.
I succeed in my endeavors.
I trust myself.
I am a competent person.
I take very good care of myself.
I deserve the best that life has to offer.

Thought Stopping

Here is another method for halting troubling thoughts and worries. This is an especially useful technique for people who engage in "catastrophic thinking." Everyone, from time to time, has had horrible images in their thoughts. Maybe they pictured a loved one murdered, or thought about a fire engulfing their house.

First, please understand that thoughts such as these are perfectly normal and common. They are nothing to feel ashamed or worried about, and they aren't predictors of the future. They are part of another mental habit, and these catastrophic thoughts only get worse when we try to deny their existence because they scare us. They scare us because we secretly worry, "Am I a horrible person to think about my loved one being dead in a car accident?" The answer is, no—you are normal. Just knowing these catastrophic thoughts are normal is sometimes enough to stop a never-ceasing flow of horrible mental images.

"Thought stopping" is a way of controlling troubling thoughts by refusing to allow them living space in your mind. You really do have a lot of say in governing your thoughts. The next time you don't like a thought, tell it, "Get out!" Mentally scream at the thought to "Stop!" If you chase the thought away enough times, it really will cease. Some people find that putting a rubber band around the wrist and then snapping it at the same time they tell a thought to "Stop!" also works.

Personally, I prefer to tell a thought to "Stop!" and then immediately fill its space with a positive affirmation. To me, it's a loving gift to myself to fill my mind with the mental equivalent of roses—and to constantly remove the negative weeds.

The Serenity Prayer

This time-honored prayer has been adopted by the 12-step programs as a way of reducing worry and stress that may trigger a relapse. I love this prayer, and I use it as a tool to reduce needless worry over things I can't change or control:

God, grant me the serenity
To accept the things I cannot change
The courage to change the things I can
And the wisdom to know the difference.

The Serenity Prayer is a good mantra to repeat over and over to yourself during those times when your worries turn into all-out fears! If you are worried about impending disaster, it's difficult to think clearly about possible solutions. By concentrating on the Serenity Prayer, you are more likely to identify which part of the crisis is open to your actions and input and which part of the crisis is out of your hand.

Exercise

Your brain chemistry responds positively to exercise. The increased oxygen and neurotransmitter levels in the brain help you combat worries in three important ways: you are less apt to worry about insignificant concerns, you are more apt to think of creative solutions and you will have more energy to put the solution into action.

The change of scenery provided by exercise can also help. For example, if you are sitting home worrying about having enough money to pay the bills, it may help just to get out of the house for a while. Go for a walk. Get some fresh air and enjoy the sights and sounds of nature. Meditate, or talk to your walking buddy, and you may return home with fresh solutions to tackle those worries!

Take the Focus off Yourself

Many times, we worry because we're self-conscious. We worry "Does she like me?" or "Will they think I'm a fool if I speak up?" I've had many clients compare their "insides" with other people's "outsides."

For instance, Jenny felt insecure about her looks, thinking she wasn't attractive enough to hold a man's interest. She'd look around at other women and think everyone else was super-confident about her physical appearance. Jenny was comparing her insides—her insecure body image—with other women's outsides—the illusion and assumption that they were secure about their attractiveness. Jenny learned how deceptive this comparison really is. She learned that everyone has occasional insecurities, but they are often covered up by outer appearances of confidence. Jenny came to understand that she, too, appeared to be super-confident to other women. At that point, she began healing her negative body image and reduced her worries and insecurities about whether she was "attractive enough."

Another client, Suzanne, was worried about an upcoming public speech her employer had asked her to make. "What if I forget my speech?" she worried. "What if I make a fool of myself and everyone laughs at me?"

Public speaking is one of the most common fears among adults, if not the most common fear. Together Suzanne and I worked on having her de-focus on herself. She trained her thoughts to focus on other parts of the speaking engagement. Suzanne concentrated on a mental image of the audience members smiling as she shared valuable tips and information with them. Suzanne told herself how much she'd be helping others by giving them useful data and suggestions. And by focusing on how much her speech would help others, Suzanne was able to reduce her worries and self-consciousness considerably. By the way, her speech went off without a hitch,

and she received thunderous applause from the audience. After-
ward, she told me, "That was fun! I can't wait to do it again!"

Take Action to Make Things Better

Are you worried that your car will break down? Then get it
repaired or tuned up now! Are you worried that you'll run out of
money? Then figure out a way to increase your income or reduce
your expenses. Are you worried you'll get sick and be unable to
work? Then get a medical checkup and learn about (and practice)
behaviors that prevent or reduce the risk of disease.

You really do have quite a bit of control over your finances,
health, career, education and life circumstances. If you are worried
about something, the best course of action is to do something to fix
it. This can be frightening—especially if it involves risking failure
or making major life changes. But which is worse? Taking action or
worrying yourself to death?

Research shows that the most important part of increasing your
self-esteem is feeling competent and that you have a sense of mastery over your life. Self-esteem has little to do with your age,
income, where you live, what type of car you drive or how much
education you have. What self-esteem does involve is being self-
reliant. If you don't like your life, then you must take steps to
change it to suit your expectations. You will be happier, and this
will positively affect those around you.

Think of Worst-Case Scenarios

The next time you're worrying, ask, "What's the worst thing
that could happen?" By mentally facing that possibility, you'll
immediately feel a greater sense of control. The answer may be
frightening, because the worst thing could be a horrible prospect,
involving financial or physical ruin. But keep going. Ask yourself
whether the sky would fall down in this worst-case scenario. You
will find the inner strength to handle any challenge.

Develop a Fatalistic Philosophy

We can control a great deal of our lives, yet there are some parts that are out of our control—an airplane trip, for example. You have complete control over where you are flying and when, and what airline and airport you use. Even if your job depends on your being on that plane, you have the right to refuse to board the airplane, if that is what you really want.

But once you strap yourself into seat 15A and the plane takes off into the air, you are sharing control of your life with several other people—namely, the pilot and the air traffic controller. How do you handle worry in such a situation? How do you stop thoughts about death and disaster when the control is out of your hands?

You can develop a fatalistic philosophy at that point that says, "Everything happens for a reason. When my time has come to die, it will come. If it's not yet time for me to die, I will survive a plane crash." Many people find this belief in fate to be very comforting. It allows them to trust that some higher plan is in action, and that a divine will is being conducted as they travel (hopefully, safely) through the air.

Condition Yourself to Relax

I've worked with a lot of clients who had phobias of airplane travel. It actually became a clinical sub-specialty of mine, because I had so many clients requesting this treatment. A television station even asked me to perform an airplane phobia treatment on a news-woman who really was afraid of travelling. We went through three sessions, in front of the cameras, to enable this woman to go on a long-awaited honeymoon trip via airplane. (She did it!).

In formal therapy sessions, I take clients through a very involved process of progressive relaxation. This is paired with images associated with flying, and gradually the two images—being relaxed and being in an airplane—are fused, and the client is able to have a pleasant, relaxed airplane trip.

You can do a version of this therapy for yourself. And you can use it to stop chronic worries. Here's a great technique to try:

First, go somewhere alone (such as your bedroom or in a bubble bath) where you won't be disturbed for about thirty minutes. Take the phone off the hook and put a "Do Not Disturb" sign on the door. Get as comfortable as possible.

Either by listening to a progressive relaxation cassette tape or by mentally telling your muscles, one by one, to let go and relax, give yourself permission to rest for thirty minutes. Take deep breaths and concentrate on the sound of your breathing and notice as your heart rate slows. Breath in and out, very deeply. Each time you exhale, let go of any worries or cares. As you inhale, breathe in delicious feelings of relaxation. Let go, and give in to the wonderful feeling of deep relaxation.

Then, go on a mental vacation. Since the trip is free of charge, you'll want to choose a wonderful place such as a tropical island, a peaceful garden, a beautiful lake or a woodsy mountain cabin. Anywhere you feel good and relaxed is fine. Keep breathing in and out deeply as you become more and more relaxed.

Next, put your right thumb and index finger together to form a circle. Hold that circle while you enjoy your relaxation and vacation paradise. Enjoy the relaxation as long as you want, for a minimum of thirty minutes. Make sure to keep your thumb and index finger together in a circle.

You may want to repeat this exercise two or three more times to really strengthen the power of this technique.

Now, here's how to put this method into action: you have taught yourself to relax instantly whenever you put your thumb and forefinger together. Whenever you have a worrisome thought, you can pull out this powerful tool! Simply form a circle with your thumb and forefinger and notice how you instantly feel more calm and self-assured.

Declare Your Freedom from Guilt and Worry 59

All these techniques will help you combat worrying and fretting through positive action!

CHAPTER SIX

Shades of Anger

Many of my clients entered therapy holding onto a lot of anger toward some "perpetrator" who was responsible for ruining their lives. These women would complain that "if only it weren't for (my father, my mother, my husband, my children, etc.), then my life would have been different. I would have had my wishes fulfilled, and I'd be happy today."

Belinda blamed her husband for blocking her goal of getting a college education. Rhonda resented her father for dying twenty years earlier, when she was a teenager, leaving the family in such financial ruin that Rhonda had to quit the cheerleader squad and take an after-school job. Patty told me that if it weren't for her children, she would be able to fulfill her dream of being a professional photographer.

Frustration, Bitterness and Resentment

Belinda, Rhonda, and Patty all had suffered, but not because of outside forces. Their suffering was a product of their thoughts about the situation. Thoughts that led to corrosive emotions: bitterness and resentment.

In therapy, Belinda realized that she could go to college any-time she really wanted to. No one—not her husband or anyone else—could prevent her from achieving her goals. The real reason Belinda hadn't enrolled in college was her deep fear of failing a class. She decided to take a course designed to help adults enroll in college after years of being out of school. This course boosted Belinda's confidence in her studying and test-taking skills, and the next semester she enrolled in three classes.

Like Belinda, Rhonda had put her goals, hopes and dreams on hold. She held onto resentment toward her late father for dying and taking away her upper-middle-class lifestyle. Rhonda was "stuck" in the anger stage of the grieving process, and we spent months work-ing through her mixed emotions. Rhonda wrote letters to her late father, and we'd read the heartfelt words in our sessions. Gradually her rage and tears were replaced with a new determination to move forward in pursuing her goals. Rhonda put more energy and enthu-siasm into her work and received a promotion and a raise.

Patty's resentment toward her children was also misplaced. She told me of her long-held desire to be a photojournalist, traveling with *National Geographic* caravans to exotic jungles. That venture is unrealistic for a mother of two toddlers, so Patty and I searched for ways to get her creative needs met, as well as take care of her mater-nal responsibilities.

She assembled a portfolio of her best photography and was hired for a part-time position at a locally published magazine. Patty did her photography work in the morning while her children were at preschool and was home with them in the afternoon. Occa-sionally, when her photography assignments would interest the children—like the time she covered a circus that had come to town—she'd bring her toddlers along with her. Patty told me that when the kids are in college, she just may get a position with *National Geographic* after all.

Jealousy and Envy

Like shame and guilt, jealousy and envy are often misconstrued as interchangeable terms. According to researchers W. Gerrod Parrott, Ph.D., of Georgetown University and Richard H. Smith, Ph.D., of the University of Kentucky, envy means we desire what someone else has—her car, her great figure or her glamorous profession. Jealousy, say Parrott and Smith, occurs when we feel threatened with losing something or someone valuable to us.

We may envy that gorgeous woman with her knockout figure, beautiful gown and easygoing attitude at the company party. But we feel jealous when she begins talking to our boyfriends, because we fear they'll find her more attractive and will abandon us for her.

Parrott and Smith claim that jealousy is a more socially acceptable emotion than envy. But as a psychotherapist, I believe jealousy is a more difficult emotion to deal with than envy.

After all, what do you do when you feel jealous because your boyfriend is talking with Ms. Gorgeous? For a lot of women, that sort of situation presents a dilemma: do you confront your boyfriend about flirting and risk appearing petty and insecure? Do you latch your arm around your boyfriend as he's talking with Ms. Gorgeous and risk appearing possessive? Do you attempt revenge by finding a Mr. Gorgeous or Mr. Big Bucks at the party and flirting with him? Do you give your boyfriend the cold shoulder, as punishment for his transgression, on the ride home?

I believe jealousy stems from two bases: anger and fear of abandonment and rejection. We will learn healthy ways to express anger in the next section.

Fears of abandonment and rejection can come from a number of sources. Sometimes they have to do with the deep-seated feelings of shame discussed earlier in this chapter. When this is the case, psychotherapy is the most useful prescription for ridding yourself of these life-ruining ghosts from the past.

Fear of rejection and abandonment can also stem from unhealthy relationship patterns. If you have a history of having men leave you, then of course you are bound to fear being abandoned again! Again, therapy can help. Most women who have been involved in numerous destructive relationships are blind to how they alone are responsible for choosing emotionally unhealthy men. A good therapist can help in identifying, and in healing, this pattern.

Finally, fears of rejection and abandonment can stem from not living up to your potential. In other words, if you are taking the time to fulfill your emotional, physical and career goals, you will feel secure and happy with yourself. There is no need to feel uneasy about Ms. Gorgeous talking with your boyfriend because you know you will be okay no matter what happens. You feel secure in your healthy relationship with your boyfriend because you picked an emotionally healthy man to get involved with. You also know that—worst case—if your boyfriend were to elope with this woman tomorrow, your life wouldn't fall to pieces. Self-fulfillment really is your best insurance against feeling jealous, insecure and afraid.

Envy—when you desire someone else's profession or lifestyle—can actually produce positive experiences! For example, many of my clients were unclear about their goals when they entered therapy. So I'd ask them to brainstorm with me about every instance they could remember when they felt envious of another person.

At age 34, Tammy needed to get a job for the first time in her life. Her husband had asked for a divorce and the judge had awarded only one year's alimony to Tammy. Within one year, Tammy needed a way to support her two young children.

With no formal occupational training, Tammy knew she needed to go to school to learn a profession but was unsure of what kind of job would make her happiest. I asked her to tell me about all the people she'd ever envied, and this question triggered a wave of emotion and information. She spoke rapidly and enthusiastically about how she'd always envied lawyers, authors, judges and journalists. I asked her why she envied these positions, and I wrote down every bit of information she discussed.

This brainstorming session produced a clear picture of Tammy's inner desires to work in the legal profession. Since Tammy needed to produce an income within one year, when her husband's alimony would stop, she didn't have time to go to law school (although that was an option for her later). We discussed all aspects of legal careers—lawyer, legal secretary, paralegal, law clerk, court reporter. As soon as I said, "court reporter," Tammy practically leaped out of her chair and exclaimed, "Yes, that's it! I've always wanted to be a court reporter!" She enrolled in court reporting school the next day. Tammy had reframed "envy" into a tool for listening to her deepest desires about careers.

Envy is considered a hot-potato emotion. It's a feeling many people feel uncomfortable in admitting, because of childhood or religious messages that we shouldn't feel envy. True, envy is unpleasant. Envy can also be very destructive and damaging if you let its bad feelings poison your soul.

But I believe that everyone, from time to time, experiences fleeting moments of envy. I think that envy, like every emotion that humans experience, has a meaning and purpose. The question isn't whether or not you have envy, but what you do with it.

You can use—and thus eliminate—envy by using it as a tool, as Tammy did. Make the effort to reframe envy by saying to yourself, "Isn't it wonderful that she has that great car, house, marriage, figure, career, etc.? I, too, can achieve those accomplishments, and I will use her success as inspiration and an example."

Motivational speaker Brian Tracy, author of the bestseller *Maximum Achievement*, reminds us that our thoughts about other people's success can determine whether we are successful or not. "The difference between wealthy people and poor people is their thoughts about money," Tracy told me. "Poor people are angry at successful people, and that anger keeps them from attaining the success they envy. Wealthy people, on the other hand, are inspired by other people's success."

Beyond Counting to Ten: All about Anger

I think I've saved the best for last here. Anger is the number one emotion I've seen women—myself included—struggle with. This is no accident. As little girls, the pressure was enormous for most of us to smile and look pretty. Most of us received lots of messages that proper young ladies don't show anger. Boys are given a different message: Big boys don't cry.

In my work with alcoholics, compulsive over-eaters and people with other addictions, I saw more women relapse in response to anger than any other reason. These women were frustrated because they were genuinely furious, but didn't know how to express or reduce the anger.

Anger is a normal emotion, and a healthy one at that. We all feel anger in response to being wronged, and it is an emotion we can expect to feel from time to time throughout our lives. As babies, we were angry to be pulled from the comfortable womb. As toddlers, we were angry when the neighbor broke our toys. As young adults, we were angry when our boyfriends broke their promises. As mature adults, we were angry when our teenagers dented the car. As senior citizens, we were angry when the Social Security payment was late. And on and on.

So a healthy first step in dealing with anger is to accept that it's a normal emotion. If you tell yourself "I shouldn't feel angry," does the emotion go away? No! The anger, when denied or stuffed down, actually grows stronger. Fresh anger is a healthy, normal emotion. Old stuffed anger becomes unhealthy and ugly because it mutates into a hideously disfigured feeling such as bitterness or resentment.

An interesting new study from the University of Tennessee gives some answers about healthy responses to anger. Dr. Sandra Thomas and her team of researchers studied five hundred thirty-five women as to how they handled anger and catalogued how those responses affected the women's mental and physical health.

Thomas concluded that two ways of dealing with anger were especially unhealthy. Both suppressing anger and yelling, out of anger, led to headaches, stomachaches and overeating. In other words, holding in anger can make you sick and often leads to depression. Yelling escalates your fury instead of making you feel more calm.

The best-adjusted and healthiest women dealt with anger in one of these constructive ways:

- Having a rational, cool-headed discussion with the person who provoked the anger. A compromise or solution would be calmly discussed (and hopefully reached!).
- Doing something physical, such as running or exercising.
- Writing their angry feelings in a journal. This is my own favorite method for handling upset feelings. I write my feelings on the computer and don't worry about grammar or punctuation. I just let the emotions and thoughts flow out—uncensored—until I get a better grasp of why I'm upset and what I should do to resolve the situation.
- Getting emotional support from a friend. Talking to a non-judgmental, supportive and caring person is another healthy outlet for anger. Just use caution not to escalate into an "ain't it awful" discussion. Focus on understanding the source of your anger and pinpointing solutions.

Taking Care of Emotions Is Taking Care of Yourself

We all have formed habits in dealing with emotions. Very few of us have enough time in the day to get everything done, so we use shortcuts whenever we can. This includes shortcut methods—or habits—for dealing with upsetting feelings. Some people are in the habit of yelling whenever they get upset. Other people habitually overeat in response to anger.

Take the time and make the effort to develop healthy new habits for dealing with worry, guilt, jealousy and anger. Use the powerful energy within these emotions to improve your life, instead of fighting or suppressing the feelings. Ask yourself, "What can I learn from this feeling?" and then let that information spur you on toward a better life. Let it inspire you to climb that mountain, get that degree, write that novel, lose that weight or ask for that promotion at work.

You deserve it!

CHAPTER SEVEN

Someday My Prince Will Come: An Honest Look at Men and Money

Were you, like me, raised on fairy tales of white knights who ride in to save the damsel in distress? The damsel's life was rotten, even hopeless, until this lovestruck knight rode in and swooped her out of her misery:

I spent a lot of years waiting for this man to rescue me. It was such a built-in part of my belief system, I wasn't even aware I thought this way. The belief became apparent to me in odd ways.

It was one of those Sunday mornings where time stretches out in front of you, both as a threat and as a promise. One of those days when you know you have to go back to work on Monday, so you want to take full advantage of your day off. I wanted to drive to the beach and have a leisurely brunch, or go to a play or an amusement park. Maybe shopping for something really special. I wanted to seize the day!

The only problem was my husband and I were so financially strapped with bills and expenses for taking care of ourselves and two young sons that we had very little money for leisure activities. Every penny we made went to rent, utility bills and car payments.

That Sunday I felt furious. I felt trapped in our little condominium, trapped by our circumstances, trapped in my marriage.

And you know who I blamed? My husband. "A real man would make more money," I remember thinking. "He'd start a business in the garage that would make a million dollars. Then we could live in a big house by the ocean, travel all the time, and have lots of expensive clothes and furniture. Real men make lots of money because they're really smart."

I didn't confront my husband with my judgments, but I did let my rotten mood spoil our Sunday. My ruined weekend had nothing to do with my husband or our finances. It had to do with my decision to be upset. I expected him to do my job and rescue me.

My thinking, at that time, was that my husband caused me to be unhappy. "If he were making more money, then I'd be happy," I pouted like a spoiled child. It took me several years and several graduate courses to fully grasp and accept that I alone was responsible for my happiness.

At first, this realization of responsibility felt like a prison sentence. I felt alone in the world, and I felt even sorrier for myself. Gradually, I realized how much control I have over my finances, self-esteem and happiness. That's not a prison sentence, it's a declaration of independence and freedom! I don't need another person's permission to explore life's glorious options—I'm a big girl now! And as soon as I fully accepted responsibility for meeting my own needs, all my relationships began to improve. I also was not weighing down relationships with demands to be taken care of.

"Save Me, Save Me!"

Throughout my adult life, I've struggled with deep questions about money and what it means. I was raised by parents who valued artistic skill and happiness over material possessions. Dad had a lucrative job designing lunar probes for NASA. He gave that up to become self-employed. When I was very young, Dad started working out of the house.

He chose a business centered around his love for model airplanes. He became and still is very successful writing magazine articles and books, designing plans, building models for Hollywood movies—anything related to model airplanes.

Today my father, Bill Hannan, is highly regarded as an expert on model airplanes. He has managed to support our family, pay for a nice house and stay youthful and happy by working in a field he loves. While his corporate-climbing friends succumb to illness and old age, Dad is off enjoying himself chasing airplanes and writing about them.

He's not rich in money, but he's rich in satisfaction.

Even though I was young when he became self-employed, I do remember some lifestyle shifts that came from it. Before he worked at home, Mom would dress me in really stylish outfits; after his self-employment, my wardrobe came down a few notches. I didn't care that much, but I felt the impact at school. It was incredible how differently the kids treated me, just based on how I dressed! I hadn't realized my previous popularity had partially hinged on dressing fashionably. But the superficial, shallow kids made their preferences stingingly apparent and were quite verbal about it. And even though your head tells you those kinds of people are inconsequential and not true friends anyway, rejection still hurts. Especially when you're a kid.

I learned very young that money buys popularity if you want to be popular. That was my first experience with the Yo-Yo Syndrome, watching my life radically change in direction.

Our income as a family depended on Dad's editors paying us on time. I remember waiting for royalty checks to come in before we could get new clothes, new toys or go to Disneyland. I wonder if I picked up on any resentment from my mother, because I definitely formed attitudes about men and money during those years. Maybe I blamed Dad for my drop in popularity. But I always loved how he followed his heart in his career choice, and that was the greatest gift he could give me. I know he's still alive and happy today because he chose to turn his hobby into a career instead of beating himself up climbing a company ladder. As I said, I'm still trying to reconcile and understand this deep-seated attitude many women hold about men, money and support.

Can We Be Honest about Men, Money and Support?

It's time to honestly discuss our feelings and conflicts about men, the money they make and if they should use it to support us. Many intelligent, successful women have privately confessed to me that, deep down, they feel men should pay for dinner, dates and other goodies. But it remains a taboo topic for open discussion.

I was a talk-show host on a radio station where people would call to air opinions about hot topics. My most popular shows featured panels of unmarried men and women, and we'd discuss the ins and outs of dating, love and attraction.

One time, the topic turned to "Who pays for dinner?" The reaction of the panel and audience was shocking! The topic was as volatile as any discussion on abortion, racial tension or whether Santa Claus really exists, and this was in the early 1990s—not all that long ago.

I admitted, live on the air, that I still struggle with this issue. Someone said to me, "No! You?" as if competent, educated women were not supposed to harbor any confusion over the topic of men and their money. To me, this issue has nothing to do with intelligence and everything to do with deep-seated societal myths.

The Unhealthiness of a Dirty Little Secret

As a psychotherapist, I feel this topic has been buried long enough. I know, from sitting in little therapy rooms with countless women, that this issue messes up our thinking, our marriages our lives. We struggle, deep down, trying to reconcile our heart and our head on this topic. Yet, we're reluctant to openly admit we have confusion surrounding it. It remains our dirty little secret and a source of shame and disempowerment.

To me, this dishonesty about our confusion is dangerous. Until we're honest about our conflicting feelings, we'll be locked in the secret "I Need a Man" trap. Our dungeon of dependency is borne of secret fears and confusions. We wrestle with thinking "I'm the only one who feels this way" because we're afraid to openly discuss it. Let's flood some fresh air and light on this topic and look at it openly.

Why are men "allowed" to openly acknowledge they want a beautiful, attractive mate with, for example, long legs, blonde hair, blue eyes and large breasts, yet women are not supposed to acknowledge they want prosperity in a mate? Aren't they both honest admissions about needs and desires?

Perhaps women don't want to seem superficial or shallow. "Men can be disgustingly base," we think, "but we're above all that animal instinct stuff. What really matters is a good heart and a sense of humor. Women are the virtuous sex." That may be true, but I think deep down, women want it all—a loyal, kind, intelligent, good-looking man with a great sense of humor—and loads of money: just like men want a woman who looks like Christie Brinkley, cooks like Julia Child and who's a fascinating conversationalist—but knows when to be docile, submissive and silent.

The popularity of romance novels speaks to this deep-seated fantasy many women share. Have you ever read one of these books? It's like having a mental love affair with a man who can't possibly exist. Let me describe a typical romance-novel hero: He's a little older and taller than you (so you feel young and petite), he's extraordinarily rich, handsome, generous and sweet and loves you so much he'd die for you. Oh my God, where is this man?

Romance novels are the flipside of *Playboy* and *Penthouse* magazines. Men, who by nature are extremely visual creatures, project their fantasies of a "perfect woman" onto the centerfolds. There she is, with a perfect body, openly sensual and silent. She doesn't complain or ask for anything. She is a paper doll that doesn't exist in real life.

Why Curvy Women Drive Men Wild

Devendra Singh of the University of Texas–Austin conducted fascinating research on men's attraction to voluptuous women. Singh's theory is that cavemen had no way of knowing if a woman was fertile, so they depended on visual cues.

When hips are one-third larger than the waist, it indicates the woman's hormones are ideally balanced for fertility. It doesn't matter whether she wears size 5 or size 13 jeans, as long as the waist-to-hip proportion is there.

Interestingly, Singh found that, even though Miss America pageant winners have become thinner through the years, their waist-to-hip ratio has remained constant. Every Miss America has hips one-third larger than her waist! ◆

If a man is irritated that his wife isn't as perfect as a Playboy centerfold, it leads to rifts in the relationship. If a woman is frustrated because her husband isn't a romance-novel hero, she projects negative attitudes that cause arguments or tension. In my book, *In the Mood* I discuss this situation at length.

Is Attraction Biologically Based?

I believe a lot of our attitudes about "ideal mates" are biologically based. Men instinctively crave a woman who is fertile, because eons ago, he had to procreate a lot of kids. The death rate of cave-infants was quite high, so he had to make a lot of babies to yield one or two strong adults. Instinctively, he hunted for a mate who was young and healthy enough to produce many offspring. He didn't have time for lots of dates and discussions about child-rearing philosophies. Instead, he used his eyes for cues of fertility: youthful features like large eyes, full lips, full hips and bosom and a small waist. Today, he's no longer a caveman, but his instincts still call on his desires to mate with females who fit these criteria.

Women also have built-in instincts about their ideal mates. The cavewoman depended on her man to "bring home the bacon" and protect the cave. She was a full-time nurturer of her babies and put all her time and energy into protecting the infants' health. She depended entirely on her man to provide food, furs and protection. So her instincts demanded she choose a mate wisely: He needed to be big, strong, smart, caring and a good provider. Her life depended on his being the caveman equivalent of a rich loveable hunk. And that instinct continues today.

Other researchers have drawn similar conclusions. Dr. David Buss, an evolutionary psychologist and author of *The Evolution of Desire: Strategies of Human Mating*, concludes that human males are genetically suited to promiscuity, or at least polygamy, while human females are programmed toward monogamy. Buss says that, in the wild and dangerous era of our cave-dwelling ancestors, survival of human beings depended on two things: men impregnating as many women as possible, and women nurturing those babies.

Another researcher and author, Dr. Donald Symons, theorized that since a man can impregnate in an instant, but a woman must gestate for nine months, the sexes must necessarily pursue different strategies for seeking mates and ensuring the survival of the human race. The goals of men and women are at odds with one another, yet complimentary at the same time.

Ideal Mates, Ideal Dates

Surveys of what men want in an ideal mate often yield contradictory results. Some research points to men wanting beauty and youth, while other surveys conclude men want compatibility or domestic skills in their partners. My own research in surveying several hundred men revealed that their ideal mates are:

- Good-looking. The men wanted someone who was naturally beautiful, but they also valued a woman dressing attractively and smelling good.
- Easygoing. This was the most important characteristic the men in my survey discussed. These men are very turned off when a woman complains. In fact, they really don't want a woman to talk all that much. Instead, they want her calm, quiet presence next to him—not for sex, but for easygoing companionship. Men don't value conversation as much as women do, but when they do have discussions, they want them to be positive. But men don't want women to be "yes women," agreeing just for the sake of agreeing. They want a woman who naturally sees eye-to-eye with them and who knows how to disagree without being disagreeable.

The unfortunate outgrowth of men's desires is that they often run counter to what women want. Women are highly verbal creatures, probably because we are genetically programmed to nurture children and need to communicate important information to them. Men are highly visual, again probably because as cavemen they had to watch out for dangers all around them, as well as search for food for the family.

When I asked men and women to describe their ideal romantic scenario, the answers were amazingly similar. Here is a typical response from both men and women:

We're having dinner in a very romantic place with a beautiful view of the water and moonlight streaming through the windows. My date looks wonderful, very well-dressed, and is very attentive to me. We are laughing and feeling very good, very romantic. The food and wine are wonderful. There is soft music playing in the background. My date holds my hands, looks in my eyes and . . . .

The key difference between men and women in this "ideal scenario" comes next.

Here is how a woman concludes the romantic scene:

". . . tells me I'm the most beautiful, special woman he's ever been with. He tells me how much he loves and adores me and that he wants to be married to me forever."

Contrast this with how a man completes the ideal scenario:

". . . smiles. Our eyes tell each other everything we need to know. It feels so good to be with her and know how much we love each other."

Men want visual evidence of love; women want verbal signs of love.

The Value of Money

Our ancestors were ruled by instinct—their very survival depended upon it. Cavewomen instinctively depended on cavemen for support. But we don't need to act on that instinct today. In fact, we can't and shouldn't depend on a man to provide for us and protect us. But unless we honestly acknowledge this instinctive desire for a rich loveable hunk, it bubbles underneath the surface, keeping us ashamed and afraid.

For example, take the issue of paying for dates, meals and entertainment. It's traditional for men to pay for the first date, but who pays after that? What if you make more money than your boyfriend or husband? Should you then pay for more of your dating or living expenses? What does this do to the balance of your relationship?

Men have always been pragmatic about money. Where men do high-dives into the pool of high finance and venture capital, women have historically waded in the shallow end of the money pool with "safe" money experiences such as having a passbook savings account. We stick in a toe to test the water. I think women are starting to enjoy money's benefits, but we still haven't mastered the fancy dives and swimming strokes so important to accumulating wealth.

Do We Want "Finance" or "Fiance"?

Money is more than a symbol of power. It is power. Money gives you freedom and gives you time. If you have enough money, you have almost complete freedom. No one tells you when and where to be. As long as they pay taxes and obey the laws, rich people are free to do as they like.

To me, this is the value of money. Material possessions are nice, mostly for the comfort they provide. A Mercedes rides a lot smoother and provides a lot more protection than a cheap sedan, and that has nothing to do with snob appeal. A seat in the first-class section of an airplane is infinitely more comfortable than a crowded cabin seat. Living where the views are breathtakingly beautiful enriches the quality of life.

Who cares about impressing others? I care about having a high quality of life. And what I've learned is that a truly high quality of life is possible when I decide to allow it to happen.

There's a sour-grapes myth that claims rich people aren't happy. The fact is, upper-income people have the lowest divorce and suicide rates in the country. I think this myth is perpetuated by stories of miserable movie stars, who don't represent the average rich person.

I've met people from all walks of life—famous and poor, rich and struggling. The most successful people are some of the nicest people you could ever meet. That's not to say that poor or struggling people aren't nice; it's just that people who are very successful—who know they never have to worry about money—are relaxed and have nothing to prove. They're not out to impress anyone, because there's no point to it. They are secure in their own success and competence and don't need to compete with others to prove their worth.

Yet, I know from first-hand experience that material possessions don't mean a thing when it comes to evaluating a person's inner worth. As I said before, possessions are just a means to creature comforts, and there's nothing wrong with enjoying a great car or house. But people who mistreat others to get ahead in life are often miserable and guilt-ridden, and no one you'd want to spend your life with.

Our attitudes and behavior about money reflect our self-image. If we believe, "It's up to my husband to provide for my financial needs," then we have little incentive to accumulate our own wealth. If we believe, "I'll never be financially comfortable," then we will probably self-fulfill this prophesy.

If, on the other hand, we approach finances as a reflection of healthy self-esteem, we will naturally be motivated to take good care of ourselves. We will develop healthy money habits, such as regularly saving a portion of our paychecks, keeping good credit ratings and not abusing credit cards.

The responsible use of money is a great tool to help women to feel independent and proud of themselves. It allows you to choose a man, not for his salary or station in life, but for the valuable internal qualities he possesses.

That's one of the true values of money: it buys you freedom of choice.

CHAPTER EIGHT

The Pretty-Woman Syndrome

Who can forget the scene in the movie *Pretty Woman* where Julia Roberts takes Richard Gere's "gold" credit cards to Rodeo Drive and goes shopping? That movie epitomized a fantasy based on our cavewoman instinct for the lovable rich hunk. After that movie came out, many of my clients were spurred to reconcile their struggles.

I heard many, many complaints about boyfriends and husbands not living up to the Richard Gere ideal. Women were suddenly made miserable, feeling ripped-off that their men weren't rich or generous.

Then two other movies came out and underscored this sentiment: *Honeymoon in Vegas* and *Indecent Proposal.* Both movies pitted the values women struggle with—love or money?—against one another. And the popularity of all three movies is based, I believe, on women's dirty little secret that deep down we want a Prince Charming to rescue us.

When we admit we have some ambivalence about men's roles in our lives, we can expose this "dirty little secret" to the light for examination. But as long as we deny being confused about men and money, we are still controlled by that confusion. Once we admit it and say," Okay, this is an issue I still struggle with from time to time," then we can move on.

Almost every woman knows what psychologists tell her she is supposed to believe: "A woman is responsible for herself." But that intellectual understanding is difficult to reconcile with deep-seated beliefs and thoughts that a man should financially support the woman. She's likely to feel guilty for having thoughts like those listed below. Yet, these beliefs are quite common and normal. They are the product of childhood fairy tales and lessons from parents and the media.

It's not a sign of weakness to admit any of these common beliefs and thoughts. It's actually a show of strength that you can reveal some vulnerability and confusion:

- The man should pay the restaurant tab.
- The man should take care of automobile maintenance.
- The man should buy us gifts on a regular basis.
- If a man really loves us, he will give us extravagant and expensive gifts on our birthdays, anniversaries and holidays.
- The man should buy us huge diamond engagement rings.
- The man should surprise us with first-class, five-star vacations.
- The man should indulge us with spending money for clothes or furniture.

As a therapist, I've been privy to many, many women's private confessions of feeling confused about men and money. As soon as a woman admits to herself, "Yes, I am confused," the turmoil of guilt dissipates. She feels relieved to examine the issue out in the open. What she usually discovers are three big roots beneath her confusion:

We've talked a lot about the first root—lessons learned in childhood. My close friend, Jacqueline, sums it up best when she explains, "I was a Daddy's girl. He spoiled me with lots of gifts, and I learned to associate presents with love. Today, I have to constantly remind myself that my boyfriend's expressions of love don't necessarily need to be expensive."

We've also had a cultural revolution that threw many time-honored values into a tailspin. The 1960s and 1970s produced radical shifts in our thinking about gender roles, and many of those shifts still cause confusion for both men and women.

Fun deprivation is another big root of the men-money confusion. If you are feeling burned out and your schedule seems much too rushed, you are likely to resent your husband or boyfriend for not recognizing your distress. You want him to rescue you, just like your father may have come to your aid as a child—or just like the prince rescued the princess in all those fairy tales.

Adding one dose of pure fun to your daily schedule will help you avert this predicament. You will feel happier about your life and yourself and won't want to be rescued from a dreary life anymore!

The third root is based on fear—fear of being your own Prince Charming. Let's face it, it's frightening to take on a new challenge and risk failure. The temptation is great to run and find a man's coat to hide under, especially in this age of increasingly competitive work environments. After all, if you don't try, you won't fail. But you won't succeed, either.

However, important new research tells us that the most important factor influencing high self-esteem is a feeling of competence. If you know you are good at doing something, your self-esteem will be higher. You know that you have a useful skill or talent and that you can rely on yourself.

If we lean on men to provide all our needs, we rob ourselves of the opportunity to develop a sense of competence and mastery. Our self-esteem cannot reach its feel-good potential unless we tackle and accomplish our goals.

Here are three steps to take to tackle the three roots of the men-money confusion:

1. Admit that the confusion exists, and understand where the old beliefs about men and money came from.
2. Fulfill your minimum daily requirement for pure fun, so you won't feel as if you need to be rescued from a dreary life.
3. Become your own Prince Charming by becoming proficient at a skill that is enjoyable and profitable. You'll learn specific suggestions for doing this in Chapter Sixteen.

Why I Said No to a Millionaire's Marriage Proposal

It was a strange year. I kept getting fixed up with extremely rich men. I mean, mega-millionaires. I live in an area that has a large share of successful men and women, so the odds are high that my friends and dates are well off. It was an interesting, exciting experience that taught me a lot about my own values concerning men and money.

Three millionaires that I dated were particularly intriguing. One man, with whom I became seriously involved, was a fairly good-looking European entrepreneur. He was making millions in the computer industry and was set up to the point where he didn't even have to go into the office if he didn't want to. We seemed to have a lot in common, and I genuinely cared for this man. He was extremely intelligent and well-read.

Let me tell you about just one date I had with him after we'd become seriously involved. On a Saturday afternoon, he picked me up in his BMW and took me to see *Phantom of the Opera* in Los Angeles. At the intermission, he insisted on buying me expensive *Phantom* souvenirs.

After the show, while we were eating in a gorgeous restaurant, he asked me if I wanted to go to Las Vegas. Now. An hour later, I was making airline and hotel reservations. Two hours later, when we walked in the casino, he handed me a thousand dollars and said, "Here—this is your play money to gamble with." That evening, he took me on a shopping spree at the Caesar's Palace mall. We laughed and talked nonstop throughout the weekend. On Sunday, when we were driving home from the airport, he played "Phantom of the Opera" on his car's CD player. This man and I got along fabulously, and he would have gladly taken me on many trips even more expensive and spectacular than that one.

Why did I decline and get out of the relationship? Well, he was newly divorced and not ready for commitment. He wanted to date many women simultaneously and live life to the fullest. But I wanted a long-term boyfriend all to myself, and he wasn't at a place in his life where he was ready to settle down with just one woman. So we parted ways as friends. I knew myself and my values: It would be far too distracting to date a man without a firm commitment to monogamy.

We Can Afford to Be Choosy!

About two months later, I met two other millionaires, each of whom wanted a monogamous relationship. The first one was "wife-shopping." This man, a mogul who drove a brand-new turbo Rolls Royce, was looking for a woman to fill the role of "wife."

On our first date he basically told me, "You'll do" and then started dictating the agenda for the rest of our life. "We'll date exclusively for one month; in the second month I'll give you full access to all my credit cards. In the third month you'll move in with me, and by month six we'll be married." He wanted me to move to his horse ranch in Santa Barbara. "You can buy anything you want, anytime you want," he told me.

But the whole setup was too odd, too unnatural. I wanted to fall in love without checking every detail in an agenda book. Frankly, this man just scared me to death with his need to control everything. I ran like hell and never looked back.

The next millionaire I dated—a neighbor of mine—was more down-to-earth and relaxed. He had retired from the entertainment industry, and he is a really great guy. He's still a good friend, and we've talked about having a relationship beyond our platonic friendship. We've discussed dating, living together and getting married. On an intellectual level, it would make sense for us to be together since we're good friends with similar interests and values, and we both want a permanent relationship. But neither of us has made a move toward making this a reality. I guess it's because, deep down, we know we're better off as platonic friends.

It's nice to know I have the option of marrying a rich man. But, like the cavewoman, I want it all. I don't want to get remarried until I find a man who excites me physically, emotionally, intellectually and spiritually. I don't want to enter marriage out of financial insecurity, because marriage is tough enough without full commitment and love being present.

In the meantime, I choose to be my own Prince Charming. If I want something, I go after it myself, using the three steps I described above. The price of gifts from men I don't want to marry is too high: I don't ever want to feel I'm using someone. That would rob me of my self-esteem and would erode my ability to create and write. If gifts accompany true love, then I'll accept them. Otherwise, I'll buy my own gifts.

CHAPTER NINE

Getting More Stability— and Satisfaction— in Your Love Life

I've never understood the concept of "sport dating." Yet a lot of people go on dates purely for companionship and fun. True, those are two important characteristics of living, but, personally, I want more. I want fun and companionship plus a committed relationship.

Let me ask you a personal question: Is your love life stable? Or does it fall into a yo-yo pattern of highs, lows and inconsistencies? If you are in a yo-yo relationship (either with one man, or with several), how does this affect your energy level, self-esteem and mood? Does it affect your eating, sleeping and exercise patterns?

Many of us invest considerable time and energy to achieve a happy, fulfilling love life. This is, of course, a normal and healthy desire. It's unfortunately all too common to feel like you are chasing a mirage, though. You try everything—being supersweet and accommodating, taking care to look your best, cooking great meals or buying him gifts—yet that happy love life still seems to evade you.

Your yo-yo relationship pattern might take one of these forms:

- The men you date seem to "disappear." As soon as you get close, they break up with you or quit calling.
- You can't find Mr. Right, and you keep breaking up with men because they are inappropriate for you.
- You are in a long-term relationship that always seems off balance. You have frequent arguments and misunderstandings. You talk about breaking up a lot and have actually separated from each other during your relationship. Then you get back together and it's fine for a while. Soon all the old problems return.

Any of these patterns will drain a woman's energy and zest for life! If your love life resembles a bad soap opera, it's tough to concentrate on career goals and physical fitness. And it's nearly impossible to have fun and enjoyment when you are constantly worried about your relationship's health. Women in yo-yo relationships spend more time crying or feeling angry than they do feeling happy to be alive.

What Keeps Us in a Yo-Yo Relationship?

Many of my clients in yo-yo relationships were wrestling with underlying issues requiring psychotherapy. A fear of emotional intimacy is a common reason why women enter and stay in unhealthy relationships. Robin, a 33-year-old school teacher, was afraid to get really close to another person. Her low self-esteem made her believe others would reject her if they really knew the true Robin.

In therapy Robin saw that as soon as she started to get close to a man, arguments would erupt. She took responsibility for starting a lot of the arguments, and saw how fights were a defensive measure to keep her boyfriends from getting to know her vulnerable, inner self. Robin also understood that this fear of intimacy compelled her to choose hot-tempered boyfriends. "I always blamed the men in my life for those arguments," Robin told me. "Now I see how we both played a part."

After working through her fears of intimacy and boosting her self-esteem by goal-setting and affirmations (more on those methods in Chapters Sixteen and Seventeen), Robin's taste in boyfriends changed considerably. She became attracted to a "nice, loving man with whom I had worked for over a year, but I had never really noticed before." Robin and Dave are now engaged to be married.

Another client, Delores, was in one quarrelsome relationship after another. Her life sounded like a James Bond movie as she described all the high-drama fights between her and her boyfriend. One evening, for example, Delores and her boyfriend were in an argument while driving in a rental car on an out-of-town date. She was so angry with her boyfriend that she jumped out of the car and nearly broke her leg. Delores ran out of her boyfriend's sight, and, sobbing with tears of rage, she hailed a taxi. The taxi driver ended up taking Delores to a bar for some consolation. They ended up sleeping together . . . and the story goes on and on along those lines.

In therapy, Delores saw how her thirst for drama and excitement was channeled into creating relationship problems. Like Robin, Delores had a pattern of choosing men who were emotionally immature, unstable and unable to accept or give love. Delores had a strong fear of boredom. Her contentious love life kept her from looking at herself and taking inventory of her life. As long as she stayed focused on how "horribly" her boyfriends were treating her, Delores could ignore the fact that her finances were in shambles and that she was stuck in an unfulfilling job.

Slowly Delores was able to turn this self-destructive habit around. She forced herself to take an evening-school class in business administration. She went to her bank and got help balancing her checkbook and making a budget. Each small step helped Delores feel better about herself.

We worked on filling Delores's life with healthy means of excitement—going to dinner with her best friend, enrolling in a photography class and joining a volleyball team. As she filled her hours with fun, friendship and learning, Delores relinquished her habit of having high-drama arguments. As she ended therapy, Delores decided to take several months off from dating and work on herself. "I have to be a fulfilled person first, before I can be in a relationship with a healthy guy," she told me.

Are You Ready for Love?

Delores's story brings up an important point: the best way to attract a healthy, loving and stable man is to develop those characteristics in ourselves. It's really true that "like attracts like." Emotionally healthy people are naturally drawn to one another, as are emotionally unhealthy people. In other words, if you are vibrant and excited about life, that is the type of man you are likely to attract. In contrast, if you feel insecure, confused and unfulfilled, you will attract a man who also manifests those traits.

"Don't focus completely on meeting a man," says Dr. Susan Jeffers, the bestselling author of *Feel the Fear and Do It Anyway*. "Live a full, creative life first, and then you will naturally attract others, both male and female. If we take charge of our lives and honor who we are, then we can create a relationship worth having.

"We should try being ourselves and see who shows up," Jeffers told me. "Women are afraid of being 'too assertive' and scaring off a man. Then I ask her, 'Is that the type of man you would want? Do you want to be in a relationship with a man who is afraid of who you really are?' "

Dr. Gale Delaney, another relationship expert, agrees with Jeffers. "Men are very attracted to women who are happy with themselves," explains Delaney, a San Francisco psychotherapist and author of *Sexual Dreams: Why We Have Them and What They Mean*. "Men want a woman who is filled with pleasure, not someone who is sad or anxious."

Delaney told me that men are repelled by a woman who appears desperate for a relationship. "Desperation turns off men," she said. "Nobody calls a bottomless pit back. If you send out the looks and action of a hungry woman, it scares men away.

"Be the woman you want to be and ask yourself, 'What kind of man would make me happiest?' instead of solely focusing on whether a man likes you or not," continues Delaney. "Really let out who you are. The trick is for women to not be afraid of rejection but to be grateful for rejection. If he dismisses you because he doesn't like who you really are, then it follows you wouldn't have had a good, loving relationship. He did you a favor by cutting it off before a fruitless, potentially painful relationship began."

If You Really Want a Stable Relationship, Choose a Loving Man

What characteristics are important to you in a mate? In talking with women who are happily married, I consistently find that these women chose their husbands with carefully drawn blueprints. In other words, they knew what they wanted in a husband before they met the man they'd eventually marry.

My friend Silvia Aslan is a good example. At age 19, she was mature enough to know she wanted to marry a man who was "loving, family-minded, smart, religious, generous and stable in his career." Silvia was very clear with herself, knowing what she wanted and needed. She didn't stop until she found Sam, the man who would become her husband.

"Sam had every characteristic I wanted in a man," says Silvia. "We've been married thirteen years and we're still deeply in love." To me, Silvia is a success because she approached her love life with a plan. She didn't sacrifice romance or spontaneity by planning what type of man she wanted. On the contrary! Silvia's love life is much more romantic, satisfying and stable than that of women who experience flash-in-the-pan romances.

For many women, there are few things worse than having a great date with a guy, and then privately wrestling with insecure questions of "Does he like me? Is he attracted to me? Will we have a second, third or fourth date?"

To quiet those fears, it helps to ask yourself an alternate question: "Is he a loving man, or isn't he?" By concentrating on whether he's suitable for you, you can instantly lessen some of those nagging post-first-date doubts and insecurities.

Researchers say that a big part of the phenomenon of "romantic love" and feelings of blissful infatuation is that almost delicious sense of insecurity and ambiguity in the beginning of a relationship. We feel off balance, unsure of ourselves—on a yo-yo. Some people even claim that commitment makes a relationship boring.

Yet study after study point to correlations between being in a stable marriage and having a long, healthy life. Thirty-nine percent of married adults told the National Opinion Research Center they were "very happy," compared with only twenty-four percent of never-married adults.

If you desire a long-term committed relationship, you'll need a partner capable of expressing loving behavior. Many of my clients desiring happy relationships had no prior experience with emotionally healthy men. They had no model of a "loving man" on which to pattern their search for a husband. Their fathers had abandoned or abused them. Their parents had fought nonstop. As adults, these women didn't know how to act around a nice, loving man, because they had never been taught.

Therapy, counseling or support groups (such as Co-Dependents Anonymous, Adult Children of Alcoholics or Women Who Love Too Much) are essential to break these old unhealthy patterns. It's just too difficult, on one's own, to get enough objectivity to stand back and see how and why we repeatedly fall into the same old relationship patterns. We're too close to the pattern to successfully identify and overcome it. That's where other people—therapists or support groups—can help. Those patterns are obvious to outsiders, just as you'll easily spot destructive relationship patterns in the other people in your support group.

The Loving Man's Signature Is Loving Behavior

Patty and Greg had dated for two months, and he still hadn't used the "L" word. Patty was sure she was in love with Greg, but did she dare tell him? In my national survey of men, I discovered important information Lisa should know before declaring her feelings to Greg.

First, men express their feelings through actions. Because of biological and social upbringing differences, men don't use as many words as women to convey what they think and feel. If they like or love a woman, they show it. Men across the country told me they feel like "fakes" or "phonies" when they use traditional, romantic words with their girlfriends. In other words, those statements we dream of hearing don't come naturally from their lips. Flowery phrases feel as awkward to him as four-inch heels and false eyelashes feel to us.

Second, guys assume we understand their "show-it-don't-say-it" language. He can't comprehend why you keep asking for reassurance ("Do you love me?") when he's gone out of his way to show his feelings to you.

The third thing the survey revealed was that men get really irritated when we complain—it's their number one pet peeve and turnoff about women. The horrible irony, though, is that we usually complain because we're unsure how the guy feels about us. We feel insecure and jealous because they haven't told us they love us, so we complain! This upsets men and they withdraw farther!

There's nothing wrong with a woman declaring her love first, in a new relationship. Many men are afraid to be the first one to say "I love you," and they're relieved to say "Me, too" when she says it first.

But before Patty or anyone else takes the risk to be first to utter the "L" word, she should be sure her guy shares her feelings of love. One of life's worst moments is pouring out your feelings, only to be met with an awkward silence and a blank stare on his face.

So how can you be sure whether your man loves you or not? Here are the top ten ways males convey their sincere feelings of love. If he displays at least eight of these behaviors, it's a pretty safe bet he's in love with you!

1. He Calls or Sees You Every Day

When you're in love, you want to spend as much time as possible with the other person. Boyfriend and girlfriend become best friends, doing activities together and telling each other everything. Of course, there will be those occasional days when he has to be out of town. But, in general, a guy in love will make daily contact with the object of his affections.

2. He Stares into Your Eyes, and His Pupils Get Bigger

Research shows that everyone, from babies to elderly people, stares at people they love. Interestingly, our pupil size automatically reveals our emotions: When we feel love toward the person we're looking at, the pupils dilate and get bigger. In the old days, women took an herbal drink called Belladonna to make their pupils look bigger because it was considered a way to look more attractive.

3. He Doesn't Push for Sex

A guy who loves and cares about you, who has long-term plans for a serious relationship, won't push you to have sex before you're ready. A guy who loves you may even say he wants to wait for sex, even if you say you want it. (A side note: In my survey, many guys complained they don't like girls to push for sex before they're ready.) High-quality guys—the ones worth dating—need time to get to know and love you before getting physical. They also respect you, and themselves, enough to use safe-sex practices, like using condoms and staying monogamous.

4. When He Talks about the Future, He Talks about "Us" or "We"

If he includes you in his future plans, he's showing his intentions of having a long-term relationship with you. He's serious about you and the relationship, and that level of seriousness comes from one source: love.

5. He Introduces You to His Friends and Family (especially if he introduces you as his "girlfriend")

If he loves you, he'll naturally want to bring you into his world. As his girlfriend and best friend, he wants you to hang out with his circle of pals. He may also want feedback from his friends, to see whether they like and approve of you, too. But don't worry too much about impressing others. If he's truly in love with you, it'll be hard to sway his feelings.

6. He Swallows Hard When He's with You

Like dilating pupils, the Adam's apple and swallowing reflex reveals our emotions. If, when he's talking with you or kissing you, he swallows so hard that you can see and hear the gulp, that's a sign he's feeling strong emotions toward you (like love!).

7. He Accompanies You to Places or Activities He Normally Wouldn't Attend

Does he offer to go shopping with you? Does he show up at your gym practices? This is further evidence of his priorities. People in love think it's important to spend time together, even if it means waiting outside the dressing room while you try on clothes.

8. He Lets You Know Your Relationship Is Special or Different

A guy in love sometimes "talks around" the "L" word. He'll tell you he loves you in so many words. Here are some examples: "I've never met anyone like you before," "You're so easy to talk to," "I feel so comfortable around you," or "You're different from all the other women I've met." He also signals he doesn't want your relationship to end by saying things like, "I want us to always be together."

9. He Performs Little Chivalrous Acts

Another sign of his affection is the romantic behavior he displays around you. This includes opening doors for you, defending you, carrying things for you and holding your hand. He also reveals his true feelings by changing his personal habits. Suddenly he's dressing better, combing his hair or wearing cologne. Newly-in-love guys are also prone to nervous clumsiness because they're so self-conscious about making a good impression on you.

10. He Treats You with Respect

Although last on this list, this behavior is number one in importance. If he really loves you, if he's a guy worth investing your time and feelings, then he'd better treat you right. Signs of respect include listening to your opinions and never putting you down or belittling you. He may tease you now and then—as lovers often do—but he never teases to the point of hurting your feelings. In other words, he shows his love by treating you with love.

CHAPTER TEN

Twenty Things a Smart Woman Never Says to a Man

Patricia's wedding was beautiful, the result of much work and planning. Unfortunately, she hadn't put as much forethought into her wedding night, and it turned into a disaster. Patricia was exhausted, and in her tired state she made an offhand remark to her new husband. The remark set him off and killed the romantic feelings created by their wedding.

Many women, like Patricia, learn the hard way that certain phrases upset men, leading to major misunderstandings. Just as women hate criticisms about their weight, men have "hot buttons" all their own. When his buttons are pushed by her words, he reacts by pulling away. He may become aloof, irritable or angry. The couple then misses out on closeness and harmony.

Keep your marriage on a positive note, beginning with your very first day as husband and wife. To avoid needless arguments, misunderstandings and hurt feelings, never do the following.

1. Compare Him with Other Men

This was the number-one subject men told me they hate to hear from their wives or girlfriends. Even if you're comparing him positively to someone else, men still don't like it! Negative comparisons—"Why can't you be more affectionate, like Tom?"—are especially guaranteed to upset him.

2. Talk about Your Ex-Boyfriends

He doesn't want reminders that you've been in another guy's arms. Even a seemingly complimentary remark like "you're so much more romantic than my ex-boyfriend" can be upsetting to many men.

3. Insult or Joke about His Body

Men, like women, take remarks about their hair, private parts and body tone very personally. To you, it may seem like an innocent comment about the size of his stomach. To your husband or boyfriend, such a remark can be deeply wounding.

4. Offer to Show Him How to Do Something "Correctly"

Men see themselves as strong and smart. If you play the role of teacher with him, he'll feel less of a man. You don't have to play dumb around him, but do let him figure out how to hook up the VCR on his own!

5. Insult or Put Down His Mother—Even If He Does!

His mother is off limits when it comes to teasing. If you have gripes about your mother-in-law, save them for your best friend.

6. Mention the "D" Word (Divorce), or Threaten to Leave Him or Have an Affair

This introduces the thought, or possibility, that you could split up. These threats never bring positive results. Instead, they are the equivalent of pouring poison on your relationship. If you are frustrated or angry, talk directly about the issues with him.

7. Correct or Belittle Him in Public

Your husband or boyfriend desperately wants to be your hero. To feel hero-like, he needs to be admired and respected by you, especially around others. The nice thing is if you treat him like a hero, he'll reward you by acting like your hero.

8. Lie to Him or Break Promises

If he stops trusting you, he'll probably react by holding back affection and romantic gestures. You don't want that! Do your best to keep trust intact.

9. Give Him an Ultimatum

Men rebel against being forced or controlled. If you give him an ultimatum, he may, out of defiance, choose the option that destroys your marriage. Don't put him into that position.

10. Say "Do You Wish You Were with Her Instead of Me?"

Jealousy is a normal reaction when we fear losing the one we love. But unless your husband has lipstick on his collar or shows other classic signs of unfaithfulness, don't inflict your jealousy on him. Jealousy confuses and irritates men. Your husband can't understand why you feel insecure. To him, the ultimate expression of his love is the fact that he married you.

11. Talk to Him When His Favorite Team Is Playing

Let him enjoy being completely absorbed by the baseball game on television. And never ask him a question during a touchdown, free throw or home run.

12. Tell Him He Can't Spend Saturday Playing Golf, Softball, Tennis, etc.

As long as his hobbies aren't creating financial hardships or taking him away from you more than two days a week, don't interfere with them? Remember that men hate to be controlled. He wants you to be his wife or girlfriend, not his mother. Your man also needs play time to relax and feel fulfilled. And a relaxed, fulfilled man is nice to be around! You should have hobbies or interests of your own, or consider joining him in his favorite activities.

13. Manipulate or Pressure Him

If you want something, there's only one healthy way to get it: ask directly for it. If he doesn't comply, talk with him until you understand his reasoning. Then share your own reasons and feelings with him. Once you understand each other's positions, you can create solutions.

14. Talk Condescendingly or Sarcastically to Him

If you are angry about something, confront that issue directly. Pent-up anger is often disguised as sarcasm, and the results can be lethal to love and romance. He'll sense your rage, but unless he understands it, he can't fix what's really bothering you.

15. Try to Make Him Jealous

Jealous men pull away from their mates, not toward them.

16. Curse at Him or Call Him Names

Those words said in the heat of anger will echo in his mind.

17. Fail to Apologize When It's Warranted.

18. Imply he's a failure

When he's down or has a problem, he needs your emotional support. Tell him you believe in him, and he'll believe more in himself.

19. Say You're Unhappy Because You Want More Money, a Bigger House, a Better Car, etc.

He'll take this personally and feel he's let you down. If his self-esteem is lowered, he's less apt to be financially successful.

20. Fail to Say, "I Love You"

This magical phrase reinforces all those feelings that made you fall in love and get married in the first place.

Taking Charge:

Getting More Stability in

Your Physical Life

ABOUT PART THREE: YOUR PHYSICAL LIFE

Check back to the self-quiz in Chapter Two. If you scored three or fewer true answers to Section Two, you are in the majority. Most women have low scores in Section Two; it's rare for anyone to answer True to more than six questions in the section about physical fitness.

Most—maybe all—women are dissatisfied with their bodies. Even world-class athletes and professional models think they are "flawed." I've had women in my psychotherapy practice who were stunning—downright gorgeous—yet every one of them told me she disliked some part of her body—her nose, her thighs, her breasts or her rear end.

Survey after survey points to women's dissatisfaction with their figures. Many theories blame media messages for this collective mental eating-disordered thinking. Magazines, movies, television—all apply the pressure to conform to confusing beauty ideals and make us nervous that we're not living up to our physical potential.

After years of dieting madness, many women are learning how to relax and attain peace with themselves concerning their bodies, weight and figures. In my books, *The Yo-Yo Syndrome Diet* and *Losing Your Pounds of Pain*, I address this topic in depth.

Giving Your Physical Life the Attention It Deserves

When our schedules get crammed full of business meetings, little-league playoffs and holiday gatherings with family and friends, what's the first area of our life we rob in order to get extra time? Right! We let go of that little bit of time we had allocated for exercise and sleep.

Exercise isn't always the most pleasant activity. Although some parts are more fun than others, I really don't like exercising. Once I'm in the middle of exercising, it's a fairly pleasant activity. But given the choice between going to the movies or strapping on my inline roller skates, it's clear to me that I don't have to force myself to go the movies. But there are many days I have to force myself to start exercising.

So, okay, I admit it—I really don't like exercising, but I love having exercised! The feeling of well-being and energy after a workout is wonderful. Exercise is such an incredibly powerful stress-management tool that I can't imagine life without it. If I did not exercise, I couldn't possibly accomplish all my goals.

Yet, because exercise itself isn't always all that much fun, it's easy to abandon when schedules get tight.

And then there's sleep, glorious sleep. This central component of our physical life is so important, yet so taken for granted. Without enough quality sleep, we feel tired and dragged down. Fatigue can ruin a day.

In Part Three, we'll discuss ways to take charge of your exercise program and sleep habits. You'll read methods for incorporating fitness into a super-busy schedule and tips for getting a great night's sleep. You'll hear from experts in physical fitness, physiology and sleep medicine.

Your physical life, like your emotional and intellectual life, is definitely an area where you have to decide to take charge. Once you make that decision, the methods outlined in Part Three will help you creatively incorporate a healthy physical life into your busy schedule.

CHAPTER ELEVEN

Is Your Life on Hold While You Wait to Lose Weight?

Twenty-eight-year-old Melissa wanted to be loved and get married. She thought losing seventy-five pounds was her ticket to the altar. But Melissa's focus on weight and marriage was misdirected. In therapy, she discovered that happiness and attractiveness had little to do with marriage—and nothing to do with weight.

Here's what Melissa said two months after beginning therapy. "I see now how I had put my whole life on hold, believing I had to lose weight before I could find love or happiness. I see now that I was postponing living!"

Melissa began putting energy into fulfilling her goals, and the transformation in her outlook and appearance was staggering. Three months into therapy, two slender female coworkers asked Melissa to join them at a dance. At one time, Melissa avoided situations where she might feel rejected because of her size. But now Melissa was feeling good about herself, so she put on her prettiest outfit and joined her friends. And guess what happened? Melissa was asked to dance practically every number!

Are you missing opportunities to enjoy life and love because of beliefs about your size or weight? It's so easy to internalize negative attitudes of society concerning large women. Without realizing it, we harbor self-hatred because we are large. This self-hatred is then displayed in our mannerisms, facial expressions—even the way we walk. We become neon signs advertising, "I don't like myself!"—and then wonder why others aren't attracted to us.

Why Dieting Harms Self-Esteem

The whole idea of "dieting" is centered around negativity. The premise of a diet is to "lose," "get rid of," and "eliminate" some "bad" part of the body. You begin a diet thinking you are defective (too fat), and need to fix yourself (lose weight). There is nothing wrong with wanting to improve your health, of course. But when we internalize the negative messages of dieting that tell us we are inferior or bad, how can we possibly feel good about ourselves?

Are You Postponing Happiness?

Sometimes we feel undeserving of good things in life, thinking, "First, I'll lose weight, then I'll start on my goals." Don't put your life on hold! Here are signs of postponing happiness:
1. Wanting to go to school but not making the time.
2. Feeling jealous of others who seem to have happier lives.
3. Telling yourself, "After I lose weight, then I'll start on my goals."
4. Thinking, "If it weren't for my (spouse, parents, job, weight, etc.), then my life would be perfect."
5. Thinking, "If I win the lottery, or get a windfall, then I'll start pursuing my dreams."
6. Believing you don't have time to work on your goals.

I've worked with many women who told me, "If only I could lose weight, then the rest of my life would be perfect." Their lives were on hold, pending this weight loss. Many of my clients harbored negative self-images, believing they weren't "good enough" for love, wealth and happiness because of their large bodies. They didn't believe they deserved anything good, so they denied themselves the opportunities where good could come to them. But when they could begin to love themselves, so could others.

Melissa, for example, was love-starved when she came to me for psychotherapy. Convinced her lack of love stemmed from her large size, she walked around like a beaten puppy with her tail between her legs. Every ounce of Melissa's body language exuded the message, "I'm unlovable."

I put Melissa on a "mental diet," purging her negative self-concepts and self-defeating attitudes. I told her love doesn't have to come from a man (men can actually be the worst source of love!). Instead, you can feel love by developing friendships, attending

7. Fearing your family and/or spouse will leave you or reject you if you pursue your ambitions.
8. Thinking, "I'll be so old by the time I reach my goal."
9. Waiting for some authority figure to give you permission to start your goals.

While these beliefs can seem well-founded, they are actually based on deep fears of failure. The goal seems so big, it's like facing a mountain! To conquer this fear, break the goal into extremely small pieces and accomplish them baby step by baby step. For example, if you want to go to school, begin by calling the school to get an appointment with a curriculum counselor who will advise you which courses you need to take. Next, go to the appointment. Then, sign up for your classes. This is how all goals are reached—bit by bit.◆

church, reading great books, playing with animals, appreciating nature's beauty and using affirmations.

Inner attractiveness comes from feeling love and from embracing life's excitement and the exhilaration of pursuing a goal. When you are turned on by living, the expression on your face and in your body language signals others that you are a dynamic, alive person. You are irresistible, and your energy is infectious!

A Mental Diet to Eliminate Negative Thinking

Look for negative phrases and words in your thinking and conversations, and try to purge them from your life. These negative words form the basis of negative thinking, which weigh down the self-esteem and soul! When you become aware of negative words or thoughts, tell yourself, "Stop!" Replace them with a positive image, such as telling yourself "I'm a good person" or thinking of tranquil images such as meadows, gardens or tropical islands.

Here are some negative phrases that need replacing:
1. I need to lose weight.
2. I'm too fat.
3. Other people deserve happiness, not me.
4. I'll never achieve my goals.
5. Love is something that happens to other people.
6. My mother (or other authority figure) told me I'd never succeed, so I guess it's true.
7. I can't.
8. If only it weren't for my (husband, kids, mother, boss, sister, etc.)
9. They'll be mad at me if I take time for myself.
10. I can't afford it.
11. I don't have enough time.

....

Ten Ways to Untap Your Inner Attractiveness

1. Say "I love you" to yourself in the mirror in the morning and before bedtime.
2. Eliminate the phrase "when I lose weight" from your vocabulary.
3. Give yourself permission to work on your goals. You are the only authority figure that matters!
4. Write down your goal, and break it down into small steps. Then break it into even smaller steps. Do one small step, or a part of one small step, EVERY DAY.
5. Wear comfortable clothes, shoes, earrings and underwear. The low-level discomfort of garments that pinch eats away at us!
6. Treat yourself like a queen. Get full-service gas; buy fresh flowers; Get a pedicure; put a "do not disturb" sign on the bathroom door and take a long bubble bath; get a massage; buy and use wonderful-smelling soaps; eat your dinners off special china; drink from your best stemware.
7. Take yourself on a date. Is there a movie you've been wanting to see, but your spouse hates romantic comedies? Go out by yourself, or call a friend and arrange a night out together.
8. Surround yourself with positive-thinking people and avoid folks who bring you down.
9. Chose to say "No" when you want to.
10. And remember, every day, do something fun. Fun is not a luxury, it's a necessity!

CHAPTER TWELVE

Does Your Exercise Program Fit Your Personality?

Regular exercisers love the benefits of exercise: a higher energy level, elevated mood, increased creativity, toned muscles, higher metabolism and lower body fat. But even fitness buffs, like me, have moments when putting on workout shoes takes more effort than an SAT exam.

I used to waste hundreds of dollars buying gym memberships, and then never attending the gym. Somehow, I guess I thought having the membership card in my wallet would magically make the pounds disappear. The reason I would avoid the gym, I later learned, was that it didn't fit my Exercise Personality.

I especially discovered that aerobics classes are mismatched to my Exercise Personality. For years I'd join gyms and buy all the cute aerobic outfits that are practically required by law in these classes. And each and every moment, I disliked everything about the class.

I detested the lack of parking spaces. I disliked the cold locker room with naked women and too-small towels. I couldn't identify with the aerobics instructor and her never-sweating forehead and irritating habit of making us lift our legs one-too-many times. I abhorred the aerobics music, which was a combination of disco, elevator muzak and unidentifiable rock 'n' roll. And I especially resented all the women in the front row who knew every aerobic movement and step. I wondered, "How did they learn all those complicated steps? Is there a pre-aerobics class they attended that I don't know about?"

But my negative attitude was misdirected. The problem wasn't petite blondes bouncing in thong-backed exercise wear. It wasn't even the lecherous men who panted by the gym doorway watching us do low-impact bounces.

Please don't misunderstand my point. Of course, there's absolutely nothing wrong with aerobics as an exercise program. For many of my friends and clients, aerobics classes are a dream come true. The class schedules motivate them to stick to a regular exercise program and they enjoy the music and camaraderie. Aerobics classes, in other words, fit their Exercise Personality.

Just as an incompatible love relationship soon breaks up, so will a mismatched exercise program. We each have nine dimensions to our Exercise Personality, and our exercise program must fit all or most of these characteristics. If we choose compatible exercises, our motivation to exercise remains high.

After analyzing my Exercise Personality, I chose an exercise program compatible to my needs and lifestyle. I learned that I have a high need for intellectual stimulation, and that without something to keep my mind busy, I get bored or distracted. So I found an exercise program that allows me to read, listen to the radio or watch television while I work out.

I alternate now between a stair-climbing machine (where I can read), a stationary bicycle (where I can read), a treadmill (where I can watch television), a workout station with weights (where I can listen to talk radio), and inline roller skating (where I listen to a cassette tape). I discovered my Exercise Personality five years ago, and since then I rarely miss a day exercising. I like exercising now, because my program fits me.

What Is Your Exercise Personality?

How many times have you begun an exercise program, joined a gym or dragged out the stationary bicycle, only to abandon it a few weeks later? Most of us have experienced the frustration of trying to stay on a regular fitness routine that felt boring or time-consuming.

In fact, the two main reasons people quit exercising are boredom and lack of time. But underlying these excuses is the real culprit: exercise that doesn't fit your personality just isn't any fun! And if it's not fun, you won't want to keep it up.

If you're a people-person at heart, why are you jogging down deserted roads? And if spectators aren't your cup of tea, skip the softball tournaments. There are so many fitness options that you'll soon run out of excuses—there's something for everyone.

The following quiz will help you uncover your unique Exercise Personality traits. After taking the quiz, decide which characteristics best describe you and try out some of their suggested exercise patterns. You may even find that you'll begin to look forward to your workout!

Exercise Personality Quiz

Circle the answer that best describes you.

1. I am at my best and feel the most energy in the:
   a.) morning
   b.) afternoon
   c.) evening

2. I prefer to be:
   a.) by myself
   b.) with one special friend
   c.) in a small group
   d.) in a large group where everyone knows one another
   e.) in a large crowd where I know one or two people
3. I love to be:
   a.) outdoors
   b.) in my house
   c.) in a nice, comfortable public place
4. When others notice or look at me, it:
   a.) bothers and embarrasses me
   b.) makes no difference to me
   c.) makes me feel flattered
   d.) a combination of answers a and c; in other words, I'm flattered by the attention, but also embarrassed by it
5. To me, competition is:
   a.) a healthy outlet
   b.) something I'd rather avoid
   c.) something I like when it's among friends
   d.) okay, as long as I'm with people I don't know
6. I often feel the need for:
   a.) intellectual stimulation
   b.) a real workout, where I don't have to think or worry about anything
   c.) an intense emotional experience
7. My time:
   a.) belongs to me
   b.) should go to my family or spouse first, or I feel guilty
   c.) is mostly spent at work or thinking about work

8. I often quit things I begin:
   a.) true
   b.) false
   c.) unless someone is pushing me to get it done
9. Spending money on myself is:
   a.) something I do often
   b.) difficult for me
10. I would never miss:
    a.) a doctor's appointment
    b.) my morning shower
    c.) my favorite television program
    d.) a business meeting
    e.) an appointment with my hair stylist
11. I work better:
    a.) under the direct supervision of an expert
    b.) with the friendly support of a friend
    c.) being free to create on my own
12. To me, the main benefit of exercise is:
    a.) looking better
    b.) better health
    c.) stress management
13. The most difficult part about exercising is getting dressed and driving all the way to the gym, track, field, etc.:
    a.) true
    b.) false
14. As far as planning my workout is concerned, I'm more apt to:
    a.) have a set exercise routine that I adhere to, no matter what
    b.) play it by ear, and decide what type of exercise sounds like the most fun today

15. I'd exercise more if it weren't for:
    a.) the time involved in getting to the gym and back
    b.) all the time my friends and acquaintances expect from me
    c.) family commitments
    d.) work commitments
    e.) the time devoted to dating
16. I've tried to fit exercise into my schedule before, but found:
    a.) I couldn't drag myself out of bed that early in the morning
    b.) I thought about exercising during my lunch break, but didn't want to get hot, tired and sweaty in the middle of the day
    c.) after work, I was just too tired to exercise
17. I've been involved in competitive sports before, such as racing or a team activity, and I think:
    a.) that competition takes away from the fun
    b.) that competing is stimulating
    c.) that competition adds to the game as long as it's between friends and not taken too seriously
18. The only way I've been able to stick to an exercise program in the past was if I made a firm commitment to working out and actually scheduled it into my day:
    a.) true
    b.) false

SCORING

Look at the following Exercise Personality traits and find the ones that fit your answers. A list of suggested exercise components or specific exercises follows each Exercise Personality trait. Choose the exercise suggestions that fit most, or all, of your Exercise Personality traits. If you're bored with your current exercise program, or if you're not working out regularly these days, then put together a routine that fits your personality.

Exercise Personality Traits

Peak Energy Time

Your answers to questions one and sixteen will tell you when you should be working out, depending on whether you are a morning, afternoon or evening person. You should be exercising during the time of day when you feel most alert and energetic. Scheduling a workout during your natural energy slump periods is self-defeating and discouraging.

Companionship Preferences

Your answers to questions two and four will tell you whether you should be working out alone, with one special friend, with a small group, in a large cluster of friends or with a large crowd of strangers. Your natural preferences about the company of others while exercising would be similar to how you feel about being around others during your work and play times.

If you prefer exercising by yourself, then isolated activities such as jogging on a rebounder, calisthenics, using a stair-climbing machine or bike riding would be best. If you enjoy the company of one special friend, then walking, jogging or tennis would fit you. Exercise involving a small or large group of friends includes team activities, and workouts with strangers would point to aerobics classes or competitive racing.

Exercise Environment Preferences

Your answers to questions three and thirteen determine where you should be exercising. Home-loving people should plan on using a workout videotape, home exercise equipment or calisthenics. Outdoorsy types will feel happier with alfresco exercises such as jogging, team sports or bicycle riding. Those who like to drive somewhere and forget about home and work for awhile will do better to work out at a gym or racquetball club.

Competitive Interests

Your answers to questions five and seventeen reveal your feelings about competition—whether you thrive on it, despise it, or like it only among friends. As with the other exercise components, it's important to know your likes and dislikes about competition. Some people who dislike competition feel uncomfortable in any public exercise activity, even aerobics classes and weight rooms. Others, who love a contest and find competition a motivating factor, should plan workouts involving team sports, racquetball or tennis. Competition-shy folks will be happiest working out alone or with one special friend.

Stimulation Preferences

Your answers to questions six and twelve show whether you have a higher need for physical, emotional or intellectual stimulation. Remember, there is no best style or characteristic; there is only the best exercise to fit you and your natural style and preferences.

People who need a lot of physical stimulation rarely have problems staying motivated about exercise. It's the other two types that have trouble staying on track. If you enjoy emotionally intense situations, you'll be happiest with an exercise program involving a deep and intense commitment, such as martial arts, modern dance or body building.

If you are easily bored while exercising, you probably have a high need for intellectual stimulation. You should be looking for exercises that allow you to read, watch television or listen to cassette tapes while working out, such as a stair-climbing machine or stationary bicycle.

Time Ownership

Who owns the twenty-four hours you are given each day—you, your family, your lover, your boss? Your answers to questions seven and fifteen will tell you a lot about your true feelings of who has the say-so over your time.

If you feel that others have more right to control your time than you do, you will have conflicts about scheduling time for exercise. You then have two basic choices: You can change your feelings to justify why you have the right to control your own time (and remember that a person who exercises is easier and better to live with, and work with); or you can find an exercise program that allows you to work or be with your family.

Priority-Setting Habits

Your answers to questions fourteen and eighteen show how you handle priorities, commitments and appointments in everyday life. It is important to schedule exercise into your daily calendar—using a pen, not a pencil—and give this time the same priority you'd give to a business meeting, taking a shower or arriving on time for a doctor's appointment.

Don't think of exercise as an optional activity that can be dropped at will—instead, put exercise into a "must do" category, and don't even argue with yourself about whether you should work out or not.

Creativity vs. Goal Orientation

Your answers to questions fourteen and nineteen say a lot about your orientation toward exercise and other activities. For some people, the point of exercising is purely to lose weight and tone the body. These are goal-oriented exercisers. For others, exercise allows people to express their creative inner selves. Remember, there is no right or best Exercise Personality. It's simply important to know your own tendencies and then gear your workouts to match them.

Creative people do well to invest their workout time in expressive outlets such as dance, aerobics, yoga, figure skating, martial arts or swimming. People with a goal orientation feel more satisfied by workouts that yield results, like weight training, body building or stair climbing. Those who fit in the middle ground between creative expression and goal orientation do best by choosing "in-between" sports such as inline skating, bicycle riding, jogging or racquetball.

Self-Directed vs. Wanting Direction and Supervision

Some people loathe having supervision while they're exercising; others feel they need it. Knowing your own tendencies may be easier if you look at your answers to questions eight and eleven. If you know you won't get around to exercising without the direction of someone else, then plan on hiring a personal trainer or enlisting the commitment of a friend. On the other hand, if you feel tense when others are watching you exercise, then you may want to keep your activities solo, either at the gym, outdoors or at home.

Finding an exercise program that fits into your lifestyle will make working out more of a "natural" activity. You won't have to push yourself quite so hard to engage in an activity you find enjoyable. The next chapter discusses ways to get motivated and stay motivated to exercise.

CHAPTER THIRTEEN

Rev Up Your Exercise Motivation Right Now!

Terry, a forty-one-year-old mother of two, promised herself, "This time, it will be different. I'm really going to get in shape!" An hour later she was at a health club buying a membership and stuffing the gym identification card in her wallet.

"I'll start exercising as soon as I get some new workout clothes and new shoes," she told the gym's membership clerk. With the firm belief she would start exercising the following week, Terry happily drove to the supermarket to buy groceries for dinner. She was so pleased with herself for joining the gym that she bought cheesecake for dessert. "I can afford the extra calories, since I'm going be exercising soon," Terry reasoned.

But Terry, like thousands of women and men I've interviewed, will probably never return to the gym. She'll find justifiable reasons to postpone working out: She has to drive the kids to softball practice, her husband needs her to pick up the dry-cleaning, or she can't afford the right workout shoes.

Sixty-four percent of Americans say they don't have time to exercise, according to a survey conducted in October 1993 by the

President's Council on Physical Fitness. Interestingly, the same survey revealed 84 percent of Americans watch television at least three hours a week. Spare time for exercise clearly exists. What is scarce is motivation.

Regular exercisers love the benefits of exercise: a higher energy level, elevated mood, increased creativity, toned muscles, higher metabolism and lower body fat. But even fitness buffs have moments when putting on workout shoes takes more effort than an SAT exam.

As a psychotherapist, lecturer and bestselling author specializing in weight, health and fitness, I've helped individuals and audiences overcome the natural resistance to exercise programs. Over the past ten years, I've heard reasons and excuses for not exercising that fall into six patterns of Exercise Procrastinators.

1. The Preparer

Like Terry, this person says, "I'll start exercising when I buy the right equipment." The Preparer spends time researching and even purchasing sporting equipment, gym memberships, exercise outfits and workout shoes. This would-be exerciser spends time preparing but never starts an exercise program.

2. The Shooting Star

This whiz begins an exercise program, but ends up overdoing it. This all-or-nothing exerciser also gets discouraged after missing a day of exercise and says, "I skipped a day of exercise, so I may as well give up the whole thing."

3. The Procrastinator

She conducts an internal argument which goes like, "Should I or shouldn't I exercise today?" Of course, anytime you allow yourself even to think this question, the answer is invariably, "I don't have time to exercise today. I'll do it tomorrow."

4. The Impatient Exerciser

This person expects to see immediate weight loss and body tone after the first day or week of exercising! Disappointment accompanies the discovery that exercise requires slow, steady commitment. This person benefits from focusing on other rewards associated with exercise, such as stress management.

5. The Lifestyler

To earn this title, this person abuses alcohol, caffeine, cigarettes and stays up too late. The next day, The Lifestyler feels too lousy to exercise and a vicious cycle ensues.

6. The Thrill Seeker

This person has a short attention span, a crammed schedule and unrealistic expectations that exercise should be all fun. The Thrill Seeker says, "Exercise bores me to death, and nothing boring is worth pursuing!"

Exercise Procrastinators experience guilt and frustration. They want to be fit, healthy and toned but need some help acquiring a "mental fitness" outlook that helps you begin and stick with an exercise program.

Mental Fitness Techniques That Will Get You Moving!

Exercise is the best tension-management tool and body fat burner there is. Yet many of us resist it. On those days when you feel too busy, rushed or tired to work out, you can actually use mental "tricks" to motivate you to exercise. Here are the tricks that work well for me, for other fitness experts and for our clients.

1. See Exercise As Non-Optional

What happens when you ask yourself, "Do I exercise today, or don't I? Do I have time to exercise today?" Usually, you'll decide you don't have enough time today to exercise. Instead, you've got to go to the bank, the store, the office, home, the kid's school, etc.

The Exercise Procrastinators who fall in this trap are The Preparer, The Procrastinator, The Life Styler and The Thrill Seeker.

The minute we allow ourselves to have a mental argument—"Do I exercise, or don't I?"—we increase the odds we won't exercise. It's important to stop looking at exercise as an optional activity: It's not! It's a necessity for achieving a long, healthy life, as well as weight control and tension management.

Would you go to work in your nightgown and say, "I didn't have time to get dressed today?" Would you skip brushing your hair, brushing your teeth, taking a shower, shaving or putting on makeup? Of course not! Those are routine necessities you create time for. Do the same with exercise.

"People make time and find time for their priorities," says Joel Scheinbaum, M.D., a psychiatrist who exercises six days a week. "Make exercise your priority and then stick to your guns to make it happen. The good news is, you'll actually have more time and energy after you develop an exercise program."

Write your exercise schedule in ink on your calendar, just as you do with other important appointments you cannot miss. Design a realistic workout schedule and then stick to it. Never cancel your exercise session—only reschedule it within the same day.

"I exercise first thing in the morning," says Tamilee Webb, M.A., author and star of *Buns of Steel* and *Building Tighter Assets* workout videos. "If I start answering telephones or get busy with other activities, it's tougher to fit a workout into my day."

2. Pair Exercise with Something You Enjoy

The Thrill Seeker needs to add fun to her workout since her exercise for her isn't inherently a pleasurable activity. I make sure I have something interesting to read—a new magazine, a book or an intriguing newspaper article. Then, I don't let myself read it unless I'm on the stair-climbing machine or stationary bicycle. I do my weight workouts while listening to my favorite radio talk show.

Many of my clients watch television while on treadmills and stationary bicycles. Do you videotape your favorite soap opera while you're at work every day? Don't allow yourself to watch it unless you are exercising.

A specialist in weight control, Roger Farel, M.D., advises patients to reward themselves after they exercise. "Put 50 cents or a dollar in a jar after each workout," says Farel. "Then buy something fun." This way, you pair pleasure and reward with exercising.

Webb keeps her workouts enjoyable by exercising with friends. "It's really motivating to commit to another person that you'll work out together at a specific time," explains Webb, who exercises regularly in spite of a hectic schedule that includes travel, taping her "Cable Health Club" for The Family Channel and writing books. "Exercising with a friend gives me something to look forward to, since I know I'll enjoy spending time talking and laughing during the workout."

3. Do the "Fifteen-Minute Trick"

Here's another great motivator for The Preparer and The Procrastinator, especially for those days when you just don't want to exercise. Tell yourself, "I'll only work out for fifteen minutes. If I feel like stopping at the end of those fifteen minutes, I will." Nine times out of ten, you'll keep going once you've exercised for fifteen minutes. After all, you've already gone to the trouble of putting on your workout clothes and shoes.

4. Set Achievable Short-Term Goals

The Impatient Exerciser and The Shooting Star abandon their exercise programs when they doesn't see immediate results. "Many people set exercise goals that are too long-term," says Kandi Maxwell, a personal fitness trainer at Sporthaven Health Club in northern California. "They only focus on losing pounds and then give up after discovering that weight comes off slowly." Maxwell recommends measuring progress by the number of reps and sets completed instead of just concentrating on how much you weigh.

5. Be Patient with Your Progress

The Shooting Star and The Impatient Exerciser can benefit from recommendations from Renee Redden, three-time finalist in Miss World Fitness, Miss Fitness U.S.A. and Miss National Fitness competitions.

Redden says the first step toward reaching a fitness goal successfully is to develop a fitness plan. "Decide on your goals in a realistic manner," she advises. "Then commit to stick to your plan for at least six to eight weeks before expecting to see changes and improvements." Redden recommends gradually building in a fitness routine.

Maybe you don't always enjoy exercising, but very likely you enjoy the benefits exercising gives you. Toned muscles, a youthful figure, high energy and a positive outlook are all rewards worth working out for. By using these mental fitness techniques, you are well-equipped to stay fit for a lifetime.

CHAPTER FOURTEEN

The Ultimate Energy and Beauty Prescription: A Good Night's Sleep!

"It never fails!" Sherry complained to me. "Almost every night, Andy wakes me, wanting to make love!"

Sherry goes to bed at ten o'clock, while Andy stays up to watch his favorite television program. He climbs into bed at 11:30, and by this time, Sherry is sound asleep. Andy snuggles next to his wife and becomes aroused, then wakes her with kisses and caresses.

"I push him away," she told me. "If he wants sex, he's going to have to come to bed earlier. After I fall asleep, I'm not in the mood!"

Sherry is right. Sleepiness and sexual arousal aren't compatible bed mates. In a brand-new relationship, yes. That's when we make love like rabbits around the clock because we're excited by the newness and novelty. But we couldn't keep up this pace year after year. We can't stay up all night making love and hope to be effective at work the next day. Sleep is crucial. Sleep experts and research show that a lack of quality sleep is detrimental to our mood, health and weight. Our judgment and ability to concentrate is impaired when we're tired—sometimes leading to tragedy. One study recently concluded that 70 percent of all traffic accidents are caused by sleepy, fatigued drivers. That's more than the percentage of accidents attributed to drunken drivers!

But getting a good night's sleep is difficult at times, especially when we're worried about money or having family or marital problems. Still, the experts say there are steps you can take to sleep better—even under difficult circumstances.

"Sleep is an individual matter," says Roger Farel, M.D., a biochemist and medical doctor. "Instead of forcing yourself to adhere to a set amount of sleep like eight hours, we all need to find what works for us." Farel says the key is to sleep enough so you wake up feeling refreshed. "If that means four hours, or ten hours, that's how much sleep is right for you."

Thomas Edison slept only four hours a night, and he cat-napped during the day. "That's what I do also," Farel said. "I take a one-hour light nap in the middle of the day, and sleep four to five hours a night. The combination of less sleep plus a nap keeps me

"Help! I've Got to Get Some Sleep!"

Does this maddening situation ever happen? You've fallen asleep in front of the television; then you wake up and decide to go to bed. You slept great just moments before on the couch, but now you're in bed—wide awake—and you can't go back to sleep!

This may be a case of "conditioned insomnia," according to Dr. Stuart Menn, M.D., director of the WesMed Sleep Disorders Center in Anaheim, California, and founder of the Scripps Clinic and Research Foundation Division of Sleep Medicine.

Conditioned insomnia, explains Menn, is caused when we pressure ourselves to sleep when our bodies aren't ready. "I must feeling well-rested."

The doctor recommends taking periodic 30-minute breaks during the day, where you can daydream or close your eyes to rest. "These little catnaps are very effective in recharging your 'battery' during the workday," Farel explained.

Sleep: Refueling in the Pit Stop

While we're sleeping, our body is wide awake and very busy repairing and replenishing the fuel we used during the day. We're like a race car driver who pulls into the pit stop for new tires, spark plugs and gasoline. In the pit stop, as in sleep, the driver rests and catches her breath. But the "crew"—the body and brain—is furiously working to keep all the parts moving safely and smoothly.

For women, one of the most important functions of sleep is a refueling of the brain chemical "serotonin." Serotonin regulates our mood, energy level and appetite. If serotonin levels are low, we feel tired, grouchy and hungry. Serotonin isn't a substance your body can store; it must be made from scratch every night.

sleep, I must sleep," we tell ourselves, panicking when we see the clock read 2:30 a.m. But the harder we try to sleep, the worse it becomes—and that's the heart of conditioned insomnia.

"If you fall asleep easily in front of the television, it's because there's no pressure to fall asleep," says Menn. "But when you go to the bedroom and can't fall asleep, it's because you've put too much pressure on yourself and said, 'Now I have to sleep.'"

Menn emphasizes that we can't force ourselves to sleep and that the harder we try, the worse it gets. "Fretting and worrying about not sleeping never helps you go to sleep," he adds. "It only makes it more difficult."◆

Vast research, such as Dr. Werner Koella's studies at the University of Bern in Switzerland and Dr. Steven Henriksen's studies at Stanford University School of Medicine, underscore the importance of sleep's role in keeping serotonin at a healthy level. The researchers explain how the brain creates serotonin, using other "ingredients" in the body like melatonin, during the rapid-eye-movement (REM) sleep cycle. You might recall that REM is the sleep cycle in which we dream, and while we dream our eyes move—hence the cycle's name.

Why a Bad Night's Sleep Can Wreck Your Diet

If you don't get enough REM sleep at night, your body won't have the chance to produce sufficient serotonin to meet your next day's needs. You'll wake up feeling hung-over—groggy and irritable. You'll wonder whether you got any sleep at all!

Not only does a lack of REM sleep leave you groggy, it also makes you hungry! When serotonin is low, your body tries to correct the deficiency by sending signals to the appetite center of your brain to eat carbohydrates, according to research conducted by Drs. Richard and Judith Wurtman at M.I.T.

Serotonin also plays vital roles in regulating endocrine glands and their production of chemicals that influence energy levels, mood and our metabolism of protein and carbohydrates, according to researchers Dr. M. Montange and A. Calas of the University of Bordeaux in France. In other words, low serotonin levels may impact insulin and other vital chemicals that influence how much weight we gain and how much fat our body stores!

The Vicious Cycle of Sleep Deprivation

"The whole world is sleep-deprived," says Adrian Williams, M.D., associate director of The Sleep Disorders Center at

U.C.L.A. Medical Center. Women who are sleep-deprived get trapped in a cycle that can only be escaped with conscious decisions and effort.

The REM sleep phase is interrupted, according to researchers, by insomnia, stress, too much alcohol, Valium and other sedatives, exercise too close to bedtime and excess stimulation from caffeine and other sources.

When we're tired because of not getting enough REM sleep, many of us tank up on "liquid energy" such as coffee, colas or tea. Of course, caffeine can't make up for a bad night's sleep. So, many of us supplement the caffeine with heavy doses of chocolate. By the end of the day, our nerves are jittery and frayed—and we're still tired! But, because we've ingested so many stimulants through coffee, sodas or chocolate, it's difficult to fall asleep that night. We're likely to feel exhausted, but not tired enough to sleep.

Some people turn to alcohol to try to get some sleep, but excessive alcohol disrupts REM sleep (that's why you feel hung-over the morning after a drinking binge). Either way, we won't get the quality sleep we so desperately need, and we'll wake up exhausted one more time.

Five Tips for Getting Quality Sleep When Life Is Stressful

It's been one of those super-stressful days. Your boss was upset, the car's brakes went out, your son's teacher wants to meet with you and your husband is pouting because you told him "Not tonight, dear; I'm too tired." You're exhausted. So how come you can't fall asleep?

It may be that you're trying too hard, according to sleep expert Stuart Menn, M.D. When we try to make ourselves sleep, the problem gets worse. Here are Dr. Menn's tips for getting to sleep on one of those nights.

1. Realize Stress-Induced Insomnia Happens to Everyone

"In times of bereavement, work stress or family problems, it's normal to have insomnia," says Dr. Menn.

2. Don't Fret or Worry about Your Insomnia

"This is very important," the sleep doctor explains, "because if you worry about your insomnia, you'll stay awake." Dr. Menn says real problems occur when we worry during the day whether we'll get any sleep that night. "That's when you start to expect a bad night's sleep and it becomes a self-fulfilling prophesy," he adds.

3. Don't Go to Bed Until You're Truly Ready to Sleep

"Sometimes we go to bed because we think we should," says Dr. Menn. "We think, well, it's eleven o'clock, so I should be sleeping." But sleep only occurs when the body is ready and our body's circadium rhythms—our internal clock—say it's time to sleep.

4. If You Can't Sleep, Get Out of Bed

"It's better to just get out of bed and try to relax, watch television or write letters if you can't sleep," the doctor emphasizes. Those activities should also take place in a different room from your bedroom. "If you stay in bed and become upset at your insomnia, your bedroom will be paired in your mind with stress and insomnia," Dr. Menn explains. "In other words, you will condition yourself to have continuing insomnia in your bedroom."

5. Keep Your Bedroom as Dark, Quiet and Comfortable as Possible

"When you're stressed, you become even more sensitive to noise, light and an uncomfortable bed," Dr. Menn adds.

6. Watch Lifestyle Habits That Interfere with Sleep

"It's important not to have any caffeine after six o'clock in the evening," explains Dr. Menn. He also emphasizes that over-consumption of alcohol can backfire and make for a restless night of sleep, since alcohol suppresses certain sleep cycles.

Dr. Menn stresses the importance of avoiding exercise after 5:00 p.m. Body temperature rises in the morning and throughout the day, and then begins to fall after five o'clock in the evening. Our body temperature needs to be cooled down to sleep, according to Dr. Menn. "When exercise occurs too close to sleep time—or after five o'clock—it heats up the body and interferes with sleep," he explains.

Taking Charge:

Getting More Stability in

Your Work Life

ABOUT PART FOUR: YOUR WORK LIFE

Look back, now, to our quiz in Chapter Two. If you scored three or fewer true answers in Section Three, it shows some dissatisfaction with your intellectual or career life. Maybe you're feeling stuck, insecure or burned out at work. For some reason, you're not getting your needs met intellectually, and this is the deficit we'll explore in the chapters to follow.

Interestingly, most people who have low scores in Section Three also have low scores in Section 1 (your emotional life).

This is no coincidence.

If you aren't having enough fun and pleasure in your personal life, you will experience an unmet human need. This creates a void or vacuum, and you carry this void with you wherever you go. You arrive at work with an emotional deficit, because your human needs for fun and emotional intimacy haven't been met before and after work or on the weekends. The automatic response is to try to fill this void at work. This creates problems at work, however, because the workplace is not designed to fill personal emotional needs.

Work is basically designed to provide two things: a paycheck and intellectual stimulation. True, you might form one or two friendships at work, and you might get personal satisfaction out of your work's meaning and purpose. But the basic human needs of love, appreciation and fun usually don't get met at work. And this discrepancy is where big problems arise.

This confusion about trying to get emotional needs met at work often leads to disappointment and burnout. It leads to codependency in the workplace. And it leads to unnecessary stress.

That's why I can't emphasize this enough: Fun is a necessity, not a luxury. We need to take charge of our personal time and get our emotional needs met elsewhere—before and after work, and on weekends. If we don't, we'll have an emotional vacuum that we'll naturally try to fill up at work. And work is not designed to fill this void.

It's so much more effective, instead, to take care of ourselves emotionally during our personal time. And, of course, to take care of our physical needs as well. This frees us up to devote our intellectual attention and resulting energy toward our career goals.

Our personal, physical and intellectual lives are all so interdependent. There's a delicate balance between them, and this requires us to make the conscious decision to devote ongoing attention to each vital area. Through giving attention to each vital area, we gain success we yearn for—fulfilling relationships, physical energy and healthy finances. This success makes the "balancing act" self-reinforcing. Our success rewards us for our efforts and encourages us to incorporate the balancing act into our permanent schedules.

This way, healthy balance becomes a well-ingrained, healthy habit—a success habit!

CHAPTER FIFTEEN

You Can Design— and Have!—the Life of Your Dreams

All I've ever wanted out of life was to be a psychotherapist who writes books and articles while living next to the water. Everything I do is directed toward this goal, and I've been able to attain and maintain my dream for several years now. On my own!

Proximity to water—whether a lake, a river or an ocean—is very important to me. It calms me and fuels me, all at the same time. It seems to awaken my soul and give me inspiration to do research and writing. Other people find creative kinship with mountains and deserts. Whatever your environmental need, I'm sure you understand how I feel about water.

I grew up in San Diego County, about forty-five minutes inland from the ocean. In my adolescence, I'd go to the beach as often as possible. I'd ride the bus or ask a friend or my parents to take me. When I finally had my own car, I'd go to the ocean almost every day. I couldn't get enough of being next to the ocean—and I still can't.

I dreamed of living right next to the water, with the sounds of the waves audible while I slept and the sight of the ocean right there in front of my window. Yet, it seemed like such an impossible dream! I thought only rich people were able to live near the water. And I definitely wasn't rich.

While I was married, we lived in the desert mountains above Los Angeles. Although I could appreciate the qualities of desert living that appeal to many people—clear air, beautiful sunsets, spacious land—I felt completely landlocked there. I struggled with a sense of being a fish out of water, gulping for air. I wanted out of that desert so badly, but my husband's career kept him locked in the area. I know now, for a fact, that my mismatched geography was a major factor in our divorce. He loves the desert and belongs there, and he still lives there with his new wife and their children.

"I Can Really Do This?": Giving Myself Permission to Have What I Want

After the divorce, I yearned to live near the ocean. But I still believed I could not afford an oceanfront apartment. I had not researched this belief; I just assumed that anything I so deeply desired was beyond my financial reach. My deep, erroneous belief was: "If I want it so much, I can't possibly have it."

And I almost let that belief become a self-fulfilling prophesy.

I found a very cute apartment one mile from the ocean. I imagined riding my bicycle to the beach, with a little folded beach chair and water bottle. The apartment was next to a very busy street, but I kept telling myself how close to the ocean I was going to be. Why, I could practically smell the ocean breeze from the apartment balcony! So I blocked out awareness of the traffic noises and put down a deposit on the apartment.

Happily folding the lease agreement into my purse, I climbed in my car to drive to my new neighbor, the ocean. While I was driving down Pacific Coast Highway, I saw several apartment complexes right next to the beach with big "For Rent" banners. These were new-looking apartments that I didn't remember seeing before, but I immediately dismissed them as being too expensive. "Anything that close to the water has got to cost a fortune," I was sure. But then something made me stop. For the first time, I questioned my deep-seated belief and decided to do some research. As I turned around and drove toward the oceanfront apartments, I tried not to get my hopes too high for fear of being disappointed.

It turned out these beautiful new oceanfront apartments were only $50 a month more than the apartment I'd just rented! Only $50 more, and I'd have an ocean view from my balcony and would realize my dream to live next to the ocean. I could do this! I could have my dream come true, and do it all by myself!

The greatest part was—you won't believe this!—the oceanfront apartments were owned by the same company as the apartment I'd just leased. They were able to transfer my deposit and lease, and I moved in the following weekend.

Once I broke through my mental block that had previously said, "If I want it, I can't possibly afford it," I had released my thinking and become my own Prince Charming. I've lived by the water ever since, and I'll never leave the water again—unless my tastes somehow change.

CHAPTER SIXTEEN

Mercedes and Money
Don't Spell Happiness

I used to do a lot of "If only-ing." When I was a teenager, it was, "If only I had a car, a guitar, a size five body—whatever—then I'd be happy." When I became an adult, it was, "If only I had a Mercedes Benz, a custom home, formal cherrywood furniture, a bestselling book, my own psychiatric hospital unit to direct, my own talk show, a master's degree, an appearance on Donahue, etc."

Well, I obtained all those things. And while they were very nice, they didn't change my life that much. People, places and things are such minor parts of our picture. Sure, a car that breaks down is a stressful irritant, while a brand new Mercedes is a joy to drive. But neither the jalopy nor the Mercedes can make your life horrible or wonderful.

My proximity to the water brings me a lot of good feelings, and it's very important to me. But it alone is not what makes me happy.

I remember believing that when I could buy a Mercedes, I'd feel on top of the world. This was partly because I was a little envious of a woman I knew who had a Mercedes. What a status symbol I thought that was! How beautiful she looked behind that steering wheel. I wanted to gaze at a Mercedes emblem while driving down the road.

I'm a great believer in using visualization to reach goals. I don't think there's any magic power to visualization, I just believe that if you concentrate on a goal long enough, your actions will ensure that you get it. So I cut out little photos of Mercedes and stuck them all around my office. I imagined myself driving a little black four-door. Finally, I saved enough money and on my thirtieth birthday, I went to the Mercedes dealer in the desert community where I lived, and I bought one.

Oh, it was great. As I drove down the road, I couldn't take my eyes off that Mercedes emblem. I'm surprised I didn't crash the car driving it that first evening. But do you know what? A few months later, driving the Mercedes had become a normal, everyday event. It wasn't even an event. It was normal. The Mercedes emblem had become invisible, because I was accustomed to it.

This isn't a sign of being spoiled or unappreciative. This is called "habituation," a process of getting used to a formerly novel stimulus. If you worked in a donut shop, eventually you wouldn't notice the smell of donuts. If you worked in a music shop, eventually you'd tune out the perpetual sounds of music.

What the Heck Is Happiness, Anyway?

It used to bug me when I'd hear the trite phrase, "Happiness has to come from within." "What the heck did that mean?" I'd ask, only to be met with a smug, knowing expression. Then, people would talk about "true" happiness, as if there's a "false" happiness implied. To me, you're either happy or you're not. I do believe that happiness is not a final destination you get to and then stop. I think happiness, like physical fitness, is something to be attained and then actively maintained.

Looking for answers, I researched the nature of happiness by taking philosophy courses, reading great works and conducting research on people who described themselves as "happy and content."

Victor Frankl taught me a lot about the nature of happiness. In his classic book, *Man's Search For Meaning*, Frankl describes the horror of his imprisonment in the German concentration camp, Auschwitz, during World War II.

Frankl was a successful Jewish psychiatrist with a loving wife and family. He also was a homeowner who was busy writing a book for publication. Then his life was ripped apart. Every single possession and everything he valued was seized by the Nazis. He was stuffed into a train and never saw his wife, home or family again. Frankl guarded the one remaining piece of his former life—his book manuscript, which he kept tucked inside his shirt. But even that flimsy possession was confiscated, along with his shirt and other clothing, when he was brought to Auschwitz.

Frankl was stripped of everything considered essential to human happiness: his wife, his home, his family, his work, his dignity. He was forced to work under unimaginable conditions, witnessing inhumanities even a horror-movie director would refuse to film.

In this unbearable situation, Frankl observed two important variables that determined whether a prisoner survived, mentally and physically:

1. Hope and belief in oneself and one's future can make the difference between life and death.

Here's how Frankl describes it:

"The prisoner who had lost faith in the future—his future—was doomed. With his loss of belief in the future, he also lost his spiritual hold; he let himself decline and became subject to mental and physical decay. He simply gave up.

state of mind of a man—his courage and hope, or lack of them—and the state of immunity of his body will understand that the sudden loss of hope and courage can have a deadly effect."

2. *Happiness is a choice we make, a choice over which we have complete control.*

Frankl writes:

"Everything can be taken from a man but one thing: the last of the human freedoms—to choose one's attitude in any given set of circumstances, to choose one's own way. Fundamentally, therefore, any man can, even under such circumstances, decide what shall become of him—mentally and spiritually."

Freedom, Control and Happiness

Is happiness a goal that can be pursued, measured and achieved in the same manner as other goals, like getting a college degree? Many great scholars and researchers, like Viktor Frankl, share the opinion that happiness comes from within—it's an internal state. Happiness isn't based on what kind of car you drive, how much money you have or jeans size. Yet, those things admittedly do influence our comfort levels and therefore are worth pursuing.

To me, the one and only value of money is that it gives me freedom. If I have a lot of money, I am independent and can get up in the morning and say, "What should I do today?" I can choose to work, play, travel or sleep in, all because I don't have to work.

I have an uncle who is very successful in the Hollywood movie industry. He writes top movie scripts and is paid very handsomely for his work. I'll never forget a conversation we once had about money and freedom.

"I have a lot of money in the bank," he told me matter-of-factly, with no hint of bragging in his voice or attitude.

"That's great! You've worked really hard to earn your success," I replied.

"Well, I have a name for my savings account," he continued with a grin.

"You have a name for your money?" Now my interest was piqued.

"Yes, I call it my 'Up Yours Fund!'"

We both laughed while my uncle explained the true value of his Up Yours Fund. "It allows me the freedom of walking away from a project where I feel I'm being used or abused," he said. "In Hollywood, there are so many power struggles, and writers, especially, are abused by directors and certain egotistical stars. But since I've got the cushion of my savings account, I don't have to take any crap from anyone. I can simply say—in essence—'Up yours!' and walk away from any project where I'm not being treated with respect."

My uncle values his savings account because it gives him freedom and control. He can control his environment by choosing who to work with. To me, this is an example of a healthy use of money. It translates to freedom.

Research shows a connection between having a sense of control over your life and your time and the amount of stress you experience. A clerical worker who is overloaded with assignments—not of her own choosing—will experience much more stress than a company president overloaded with tasks she initiated herself.

The stressed-out person feels, "I have so much work to do! No one understands that I'm overloaded, and I don't have enough time or energy to get everything done. Why do they keep assigning me new tasks? Can't they give me a break for just a minute?" This comes from all directions—the boss, the husband and the children.

The less-stressed person feels, "I've got so many exciting projects going on at once. My time is squeezed, but I'm lucky to have a career that lets me do and learn fascinating things. I'll just have to tackle the most important tasks first, and get as much done as I can."

Frankl's experiences in the concentration camp teaches us that we can change our attitudes and beliefs to feel more in control. The stressed-out secretary might argue this point, saying, "How can I feel in control when I have to do the job of ten people at once!?" Yet, as chaotic as her work environment may seem, she is still in more control of her environment than were the concentration-camp prisoners.

If a concentration-camp prisoner could learn to choose his way and maintain a sense of control, then anyone can!

In the next two chapters we'll explore specific steps for grabbing the reins of our finances and career. We'll look at the wisdom of success experts such as Tony Robbins, Brian Tracy and Dr. Susan Schenkel and their suggestions for gaining more control over our career and finances.

There will always be some parts of life we cannot control—like other people's behavior, thoughts and feelings. But we can control our own actions and get in the driver's seat of our lives. We can quit reacting and start acting. Instead of taking our cues from others, we can listen to our own wisdom about what's best for us.

We can tap our own shoulder and whisper in our own ear: "It's time to start realizing your dreams. You have my permission, encouragement and blessing. So start now!"

The Yo-Yo Relationship Syndrome stops, and stability begins, when you grab that steering wheel and start choosing the direction of your own life.

....

CHAPTER SEVENTEEN

Ten Secrets to Getting What You Want

What do YOU want? What would make YOU happy?

As women, we're rarely on the receiving end of these questions. Usually, we're asking others what they want. Usually, we're busy making others happy. Nurturing friends and taking care of family responsibilities is important. But it's also important that we get treated well. We need our wishes fulfilled, just like everyone else.

"If It's Going to Be, It's Up to Me"

Whether your goal is financial independence, political power or educational achievement, there's only one starting point in attaining any goal: taking complete responsibility for reaching that goal. Brian Tracy, author of the bestselling book, *Maximum Achievement*, and the cassette tape series, *Peak Performing Women*, says that taking responsibility is the single most important step in realizing goals. Tracy told me he believes that our passive upbringing as children sets us up to be passive adults.

"As we're growing up, education is done to us passively," Tracy explained. "Then our education is over and everything in our lives swings one hundred-eighty degrees the other direction. All of a sudden, we have to do everything for ourselves."

Tracy said this passive upbringing creates two anti-success attitudes in adults. First, there's an expectation that we don't have to further our education or improve ourselves once our mandatory education is complete. Second, Tracy senses the passive expectation that "I can wait until someone comes along to take care of me."

Both beliefs are counter-productive because they keep us from starting toward our goals. Tracy cautions us to guard against these self-defeating attitudes.

I remember learning the hard way that I alone was responsible for getting my goals met. I had just sold my first book, *My Kids Don't Live With Me Anymore*, based on a book proposal and an outline. My husband and I had driven together to the publisher's office to sign the contracts. As we were driving home, he turned to me and said, "Well, now you've got to write the book." He reminded me of the June deadline for the manuscript's completion. The profound truth of his statement rang in my ears all the way home. I can still hear it, many years later!

It hit me, in the months that followed, just how alone I was in my quest to achieve my goal of publication. No one else—not my mother, father, uncle, colleagues or husband—was going to write that book for me. I had to do it myself.

"If It's Going to Be, It's Up to Me," was a sign I made and hung in my office. Needless to say, I completed the book and many others after it. Today I have a sign in my office that reads, "Success Is Not So Difficult—Just Bite Off More Than You Can Chew, Then Go Out and Do It!"

And that's the essence of any "secret" of success you'll find. You just do it. Otherwise, it doesn't get done. If you are having daily doses of pure fun, your energy level will be high. You'll embrace challenges instead of dreading them. You'll get more done in less time because you took time to relax, enjoy and recharge your batteries.

Here's another motivation gem that keeps me moving toward success and away from procrastination: "I have never begun any important venture for which I felt adequately prepared." Isn't that great? This quote from Dr. Sheldon Kopp, author of *Raise Your Right Hand Against Fear*, assails the core of procrastination. If we wait for ideal conditions before starting to achieve our goals, we're only guaranteed one thing—never achieving them.

Don't wait until you have more time, more energy or fewer crises in your life. That day may never come—at least, on its own. Start gathering your dreams now!

Secrets of Time Empowerment

"Being successful isn't easy, but the basic underlying principles are simple," says successful businessman and author Brian Tracy.

"The main reason people feel overwhelmed is because they are wasting time at work," he told me. Tracy cited a study that separates our time at work into "hard time"—when actual work is accomplished—and "soft time"—when we're engaged in socializing with coworkers, or in personal phone calls.

"This study concluded that 50 percent of a typical work day is devoted to hard time and 50 percent to soft time," explained Tracy. In an eight-hour work day, only four hours actually are productive. The majority of soft time is spent socializing with coworkers—often with disastrous consequences.

Your work doesn't get done. You develop a reputation at work as a "socializer" rather than a "hard worker." Tracy recommends taking a firm line with coworkers who'd rather chat than work. Don't worry about offending them, just ask them to "schedule" a more appropriate time for personal conversations ("I'd love to talk more about this, Julia. How about right after work on Thursday?"), advises Tracy.

"Are these coworkers going to visit you, with money in hand, when you wind up at the poor house because you've lost your job due to excessive socializing?" Tracy points out. "Have these time-wasting socializers go down the hall and ruin someone else's career!"

When you turn your soft time into additional hard time, you'll find it's far easier to accomplish your goals at work, Tracy reminds us: "When you don't complete a task, it drags you down and you feel overwhelmed." Finally, Tracy adds this benefit of using his time empowerment technique: "There's nothing that will get the positive attention of your boss faster than if you earn a reputation as a hard worker."◆

Taking Charge of Your Goals, Dreams and Aspirations

I've noticed an odd quirk of human nature. When I meet someone for the first time, very often the conversation turns to what we do for a living. If I mention I'm an author or that I appear on talk shows, my new acquaintance reacts with great surprise and usually says something like, "Wow, I've never met a real person who is a published author." Sometimes I think the person I'm talking with feels uncomfortable or intimidated by my career.

This bothers me, although I understand it. I also used to think published authors were very different from me. Genetically differ-ent, and predisposed for publication. So, whenever I thought about realizing my dream of being published, I was faced with the giant hurdle in my belief system that said, "Only those kinds of people

Are You Sabotaging Your Own Success?

"I would be a success, if only it weren't for . . . ."

Sound familiar? Many of us blame other people, especially parents and spouses, for our unhappiness and unfulfilled goals. But these scapegoats are a convenient excuse. They are symbols of success sabotaging, or blocking your path to success.

Dr. Susan Schenkel, a psychologist and author of *Giving Away Success: Why Women Get Stuck and What to Do About It*, identifies five common underlying causes of success sabotage.

1. The Feminine Discounting Habit

Many studies conclude that women don't take credit for their successes and overly blame themselves for failures. Women attribute their success to hard work (not abilities or talents) or "luck." The only way to gain confidence and the self-esteem to accept bigger challenges is to take personal credit for success, says Schenkel.

get to be published. Ordinary people like me have ordinary careers." I felt as if successful people were hand-picked from some chosen group of people, and I didn't know how I could possibly become one of those select few.

Whether your ultimate goal is acting, singing, photography, writing, owning your own business or running for public office, it's vital that you identify and purge this type of thinking from your belief system.

Remember: Everyone who is successful is genetically identical to you and me. No one is automatically included, just as nobody is automatically excluded, from the ranks of the successful.

What is success? I define success as being in control of your time. But there are success habits that differentiate successful peo-

2. Learned Helplessness

"This is the biggest problem for women," Schenkel told me. Societal, media or parental lessons about women being "second class" lowers women's expectations about what they deserve, or what they can achieve. They "lie down and take it," like dogs who have been beaten into submission. Overcoming learned helplessness involves making ourselves take action, and not letting fears or lack of confidence stop us.

3. An Inhibited Mastery Orientation

Instead of seeing "possible" or "impossible," we see "limited possibilities." The problem starts in childhood when girls aren't encouraged to test their abilities as much as boys are. From this, Schenkel says, "Girls don't acquire mastery-oriented attitudes; they learn that difficulty and the accompanying stress are signals to withdraw. Often they find that it's acceptable to escape and

ple from unfulfilled people. Although there are many, many different important points in goal achievement, here are the ten I consider most vital to success:

Ten Secrets to Getting What You Want

1. Define Your Goals

Success experts all agree this is a vital first step in making your dreams come true. Hazy, ill-defined goals only lead to confusion about what steps you need to take.

"If a goal is not specific, you will have a hard time knowing whether or not you've reached it," advises Hyrum W. Smith, author of *The 10 Natural Laws of Successful Time and Life Management*. "You only improve what you measure. If you set a goal that can't be easily measured, chances are you won't make much improvement."

But how do you set goals in the first place? I always suggest avoid anxiety-producing situations. Unlike most boys, who are pressured to confront and master fear, girls are frequently allowed to feel justified in letting themselves off the hook. Girls who learn to use avoidance as a major stress-management strategy have less motivation and less opportunity to face stressful situations and to find more effective ways of handling anxiety." Schenkel advises women to overcome these childhood "lessons" by forcing ourselves to face challenges and fears.

4. Fear of Failure

Schenkel researched available studies and literature on female attitudes toward success and failure. Her conclusion was that "females appear to experience more fear of failure than do males. The reason, she says, is that "girls are less likely to learn ways to handle failure." In other words, girls don't know what to do with the thoughts and feelings accompanying failure. Further,

that my clients think about other people. Who do you admire or envy? What careers or lifestyles get your heart racing? List every thought that comes to mind, then look for a common thread. Do the careers you admire involve fame, money, power, being outdoors, helping others or analytical skills? This brainstorming list will help you pinpoint important qualities in your ultimate goals or career choice.

Success leader Tony Robbins, author of *Awaken the Giant Within* and *Unlimited Power*, says goals are important as a tool to concentrate our focus and move us in a direction.

2. Stop Preparing, and Take Action Now

What would happen if you agreed to have the family over for Thanksgiving dinner, and you then spent the entire Thanksgiving Day getting the turkey ready for cooking? You'd clean it, stuff it, do everything but stick the turkey in the oven. What would happen?

Schenkel says "Girls who have high levels of fear of failure in childhood will continue to have high levels of fear of failure in adulthood." Boys who fear failure appear to outgrow it.

Schenkel concludes, "Any way you slice it, a strong fear of failure can block achievement. Encumbered by it, we feel miserable and stuck. Unshackled by it, we can use our talents and our resources to the best of our ability."

5. Lack of Assertion

According to Schenkel, "Assertiveness or lack of it can make a big difference in our level of accomplishment and satisfaction with our work. Lack of assertiveness can undermine effectiveness, invite exploitation, lower self-esteem, encourage avoidance, and contribute to confusion."

Fortunately, most community colleges and adult learning centers offer excellent assertiveness training courses. These brief classes guide students through the fears and beliefs blocking assertiveness. Assertiveness is not the same as aggressiveness, pushiness or bitchiness. Assertive women get their needs known and met without sacrificing friendships, work relationships, femininity, poise or attractiveness.◆

Nothing, that's what. You wouldn't have your Thanksgiving dinner because you spent all day preparing to cook instead of cooking.

So many times, we treat our goals in the same way. "I just need to take one more class before I begin working on my goal" is a statement I've heard countless times. While we do need to acquire some knowledge and skills before reaching certain goals (flying a commercial airplane, for example), it's important to be honest with yourself in answering one question: *"Am I still preparing for my goal as a way of avoiding fears of failure?"* In other words, if you procrastinate starting to take steps toward your goal, you are shielded from

Are You Trying to Get Your Personal Needs Met at Work?

The alarm clock rings and you think, "Oh no! Do I really have to get up and go to work again?" This is a classic sign of burnout created by carrying unmet personal needs into the workplace.

When we don't get our human needs met for fun, acceptance, emotional intimacy and appreciation during our free time—before and after work and on weekends—we have a "personal needs deficit." It's natural for us to seek to fill up deficits, and most people try to fill them at work. This is futile, though, because our coworkers and bosses are absorbed with their own worries and unmet needs. They cannot meet our personal needs. And this leads to our burnout and frustration.

I often give seminars and workshops for corporations and see these classic signs of "personal needs burnout syndrome":

- Blaming coworkers for work problems. "If it weren't for Suzy in the typing pool, this job would be great!" What this usually signals is that Suzy isn't giving the emotional nurturance and intimacy so desperately craved. This is a sign that personal time isn't being used to meet these vital human needs.

the pain of possibly failing. However, because you are preparing, you can delude yourself into believing, "Well, I am taking steps toward my goal." But are you really going for your goal, or are you actually running away from it?

My client, Kathy, is a perfect example. Kathy had wanted to be a photographer since childhood. Her mother had discouraged her from this profession, telling Kathy she'd starve without having a "real" job like teaching or nursing. Kathy's mother instilled a lot of fears in her daughter and convinced Kathy that her ambition to

- Feeling unappreciated by one's boss. "My boss never gives me credit for the great job I do." The only kind of appreciation that really matters is financial reward. Emotional appreciation is a personal need that appropriately gets met by your friends, family and lover.
- Feeling that work is a big monotonous drag: "This company is so boring!" People who lack fun in their personal lives often seek to fill that need on company time. This leads to frustrations, however, because work time is for one purpose: work. While some jobs are more fun than others, personal fun time spent for the sole purpose of

shoot photos for a living wasn't realistic.

Kathy never let go of her dream. She intended to prove her mother wrong, but in the meantime her actions spoke loudly. Kathy became a teacher—as her mother wished—but she kept one toe dangling in the "water" of her dream of being a photographer.

When I met Kathy, she was "preparing" to become a professional photographer. She had been enrolled in photography courses for ten years and was a member of two photography clubs. "Soon I'll be ready to be a commercial photographer," she told me. "I'm very close to being ready. Just one more class should do it."

But Kathy had been telling herself "just one more class should do it" for ten years! When was Kathy going to quit preparing and start doing? Her fears of failing—instilled by her mother, who probably had good intentions and was just looking out for her daughter's welfare—kept Kathy from working on her goals.

3. Take Daily Steps toward Your Goals

Tony Robbins says the most important rule he ever adopted for achieving goals is never to leave the site of setting a goal without first taking some form of positive action toward its attainment.

"pleasure without goals" is a human necessity. The bottom line is if you don't take the time for fun on weekends, you'll end up resenting your job for not giving you more pleasure.

If you meet your personal needs by having fun in your free time and by contact with friends and family, it frees up your mind and spirit to tackle career challenges. The subsequent rewards include greater work satisfaction and financial gains, such as raises and promotions for a job well done?◆

This, explains Robbins, launches the momentum you need to carry you toward your goal.

As a psychotherapist, I've seen many people paralyzed by fears that keep them from striving toward their goals. The fear of failure or criticism can overwhelm you into inaction. Another source of "goal paralysis" is being overwhelmed by the size of a goal? Getting a college degree, changing careers or winning a marathon can seem like huge, intimidating goals. But if you break them into small, achievable components, they are highly achievable.

For example, I often hear this objection from people who want to return to college: "But I'll be so old by the time I graduate!" I always ask them how old they'll be in that same amount of time if they don't graduate. Instead of being overwhelmed with the whole goal, there's only one way to achieve it: one step at a time. Every accomplishment—from building a house or car to going to the moon—is built one step at a time.

Force yourself to take the time to list small steps toward your ultimate objectives. Even if you don't know for sure exactly what's involved in, for example, getting a medical degree, take reasonable guesses. "Call the campus counselor for an appointment; schedule an appointment; go to the appointment; ask about options for attending medical schools, etc."

Ten Secrets to Getting What You Want 165

Ten Secrets To Getting What You Want

1. Define Your Goals
2. Stop Preparing and Take Action Now
3. Take Daily Steps Toward Your Goals
4. Develop a "Can Do" Attitude
5. Remember the Golden Rules of Success
   - Never Gossip or Put Anyone Down
   - Always Deliver More Than You're Paid for
   - Help Others, and They'll Help You, Too
6. Take Excellent Care of Yourself
7. Surround Yourself with People Who Pull You Up
8. Listen to and Trust Your Instincts
9. Reward Yourself for Your Successes
10. Stay Excited by Making New Goals and Learning New Things◆

Taking action is important. An Oscar-award winning actress once said that the secret of her success was doing three things to advance her career, every single day. The three things could be big or small; it didn't matter. What did matter was that she consistently did three things, and she did them every day.

What three things can you do today to move yourself forward?

4. Develop a "Can Do" Attitude

In his motivational cassette series, *Peak Performing Women*, success expert Brian Tracy reminds us that everyone experiences fears of failure, but successful people don't let those fears stop them from striving for goals, while unsuccessful people fall short because they are governed by those fears.

Sometimes it helps to pretend you've already achieved the goals in order to develop an "as if" attitude. Ask yourself how a successful artist, novelist, architect, doctor—or whatever your goal is—would act, and then incorporate that thinking and behavior into your present life. You'll be amazed at how this attitude motivates you to make your dream a reality! It also gives you confidence and inspires others to help you achieve your goal.

Believing in yourself is central to achieving goals, according to Louise L. Hay, author of *You Can Heal Your Life*. She asks, "Do you believe you deserve to have what you desire? If you don't, you won't allow yourself to have it." In other words, you'll only get in your own way if you don't believe you can achieve your dreams. That is why our thoughts need to be continually monitored, and self-defeating beliefs need to be corrected and purged.

Hay also reminds us to be forgiving when we make occasional mistakes. She writes, "If a child gave up at the first fall, it would never learn to walk. Of course you won't be 'perfect' the first day. You will be doing whatever you can do. That's good enough for a start. Say to yourself often, 'I'm doing the best I can.'"

Both Louise Hay and Tony Robbins emphasize the power of visualization in goal achievement. "Whatever we focus on becomes our idea of reality," writes Robbins. If you picture yourself accepting that college diploma at graduation, or cashing that million dollar check, you're more apt to stay focused and make the dream a reality! Take a moment to close your eyes and allow yourself to see the goals in action. Add a lot of detail to your mental picture, and put in specific particular elements that are important to you. Remember that if you don't decide the details of your dream, nobody will.

5. Remember the Golden Rule of Success

The golden rule, "Do unto others as you would have others do unto you," has business applications that create success. Success experts agree that treating others with honesty and respect is paramount to achieving a fulfilling life.

There are three practical rules for conducting business that are rooted in the Golden Rule:

- *Never Gossip or Put Anyone Down.* The person you're talking about will always hear what you've said, and who needs an enemy in the company? Smart company "politicians" know the value of being diplomatic when talking about other people. If your circle of coworkers is engaged in a gossip fest, simply excuse yourself and leave.
- *Always Deliver More Than You're Paid for.* You'll get repeat business, promotions and raises because your customers and bosses will know you're a rare find: someone they can count on for competent performance.
- *Help Others, and They'll Help You, Too.* Have you ever met people who are obviously out for themselves alone? Of course you have, because there are people like this everywhere. Sometimes it takes us awhile to detect a person with this unnecessarily selfish attitude, but eventually their "me, me" nature becomes clear. Let me ask you something: "Do you feel like helping Mr. Selfish?" Of course you don't. People who develop win-win themes—"let's help one another so we can both achieve our goals"—win cooperation and support from coworkers and bosses.

One cautionary note, however. Don't devote so much time to helping others that you neglect your own goals. There's a difference between developing a win-win outlook and helping others platform, and being taken advantage of. Also watch out for the tendency to procrastinate meeting your goals with the excuse, "Well, I've got to help my boss first. Then, maybe he'll help me."

6. Take Excellent Care of Yourself

Goal setting and achieving take above-ordinary amounts of physical and emotional stamina—especially in the beginning, when working toward a new goal can feel like pushing a boulder up a mountain. The payoff is that as you achieve your goals you'll feel more energized than ever.

But during the trying frustrations inevitable with any new venture, you'll need every ounce of energy and strength you can muster. You can maximize this energy by sticking to a regular fitness program, eating healthful foods and getting quality sleep.

While exercise can seem time consuming—especially when your schedule is jammed with new responsibilities connected to your goals—it actually gives you more productive time. Exercise gives you energy and alertness, which allows you to use more hours in the day toward goal achievement.

7. Surround Yourself with People Who Pull You Up

When I decided to write my first book several years ago, I was very excited by the idea. I happily shared my dream with a man who I admired, a psychologist who was both my professor and my boss at a psychiatric hospital where we both worked. At that time, I was still very young—in my twneties—and was in the middle of finishing my master's degree. But I had an idea for a book, and I knew there were no other books on the topic. It was a book based on my personal experiences, as well as on case studies I'd collected while working at the hospital. To me, it was a logical and realistic goal for me to write this book.

But when I told my boss about my plan, he immediately shot it down as impossible. "You'll never get published until you have your Ph.D.," he matter-of-factly told me. My heart sunk and I looked at him with confusion. This was my professor, the man who'd taught me important facts about psychology and sociology. I had always trusted that what he said was based on fact. Now he was telling me I could not reach my goal? I had three choices:

1. I could listen to him and abandon my goal.
2. I could argue with him and try to change his opinion.
3. I could reject his opinion and pursue my goal anyway.

Thank goodness I had the good sense to choose number three! If I had chosen number one, it would have become a self-fulfilling prophesy. I definitely wouldn't have gotten published, because I wouldn't have tried in the first place.

Dr. Laura Schlessinger, psychologist and author of *10 Stupid Things Women Do To Mess Up Their Live,s* doesn't even try to deal with difficult or negative people. "It's a waste of time," she said. "You can't change negative people, and I'd rather put my time and energy into being with my family or working on something productive."

I agree. I also think negative people have a draining effect on our energy and enthusiasm. They pull you down and try to make you conform to their ways of thinking. ("Dream on! You'll never reach your goals!") Your goal setting and achieving threatens them—it makes them feel bad that they aren't achieving their own dreams! They want to pull you down, so by comparison, their lives won't look so bad.

8. Listen to and Trust Your Instincts

Most of us have had an experience where we listened to our "gut," or a "little voice" that guided us or warned us in a way that defied logic, yet which yielded positive results. This is our instinct. I believe our ancestors survived with this instinct and followed its path without question. We still have that instinct today, but how often do we trust and listen to it? Especially when our gut tells us one thing, and our head tells us something quite different.

Psychiatrist Viktor Frankl talks about using this instinct to survive his incarceration in Auschwitz during World War II in his book, *Man's Search For Meaning*. He describes a time when several prisoners thought they had an opportunity to escape the prison camp. All the logical indicators pointed to a perfect opportunity to escape. Yet Frankl's gut warned him not to go. He listened to his gut and was spared the horrible death trap the other prisoners unwittingly walked into.

In business, this same instinct helps us survive the traps of company politics, impending corporate problems, and other tricky situations. Intuition helps us pinpoint our goals and our direction.

The trick is learning to distinguish between intuition and willfulness (what we wish or want to happen). Intuition is what tells you something is wrong with your child; willfulness is what tells you "This lottery ticket is worth one million dollars." The first is based on a physical sense about a situation; the second is based upon thoughts and wishes. For most people, intuition originates in the stomach region and slowly resonates up to the mind. Willfulness, in contrast, begins in the mind and then makes the body react: heart racing, breathing shallow, stomach fluttering, palms sweating, etc.

If you have a strong hunch or gut instinct about your goals or business, you'd be wise to listen and follow an instinct based on a million years of survival.

9. Reward Yourself for Your Successes

We wouldn't expect an employee to work without a paycheck or a child to perform a chore without an allowance. So why are we so reluctant to apply these principles to ourselves?

We are no different from any other being—we all thrive on reinforcement and reward. You can capitalize on this tendency by rewarding yourself every time you achieve any short-term reward. This is the fun part of goal achievement!

10. Stay Excited by Making New Goals and Learning New Things

In their book, *The Success Factor*, behaviorists Dr. Robert Sharpe and David Lewis discuss the physiological principles of developing the success habit. The first time we successfully reach a goal, a new neurological pathway in our brain is created. All subsequent victories reinforce and strengthen that success pathway until the brain automatically routes thoughts and actions through the pathway. Thus, we begin to automatically evaluate every action and situation, to see if it matches past avenues to success.

As behaviorists, Sharpe and Lewis discuss how we instill or destroy conditioning. If we don't continually strive to reach new goals, our success-oriented habits taper off. Sharpe and Lewis write, "If we neglect to practice a piece of behavior, it will decline. Eventually, it is likely to disappear completely from the behavioral repertoire. The disappearance is known as extinction."

Once you achieve one step toward a goal, reward yourself, and then go immediately on to the next goal. Don't stop believing and achieving for even one day. Even on your days off, you can still be working toward realizing your dreams. Some days, the steps will be tremendously difficult; other days, your steps will be baby steps. On my days off from writing, for example, I still think about future writing projects, jot down ideas or read books and articles. Since I love my career, these steps are energizing and relaxing.

When you achieve your goal—you've got that degree in your hand, or that contract negotiated—do the same thing. Reward yourself. Then go on to your next goal. I'm not trying to make a workaholic out of you—I promise. The path of creating and achieving goals is what brings meaning, purpose and fulfillment to our lives. It keeps us excited and super-charged with curiosity and a sense of adventure.

Tony Robbins puts it this way in his book, *Awaken the Giant Within:* "How do people achieve their heart's desire and still feel the excitement and passion that comes from aiming toward a goal? As they approach what they've pursued for so long, they immediately establish a new set of compelling goals. This guarantees a smooth transition from completion to new inspiration and a continued commitment to growth. Without that commitment, we'll do what's necessary to feel satisfied but never venture outside our comfort zones. That's when we lose our drive: We lose our desire to expand and we begin to stagnate. Often people die emotional and spiritual deaths long before they ever leave their physical bodies."

CHAPTER EIGHTEEN

Finally!
A Stress-Management
Strategy That Really
Works

"The boss wants to see you," Charleen told her coworker, Suzanne. "He said it's urgent and he needs to see you now."

Suzanne swallowed hard and caught her breath as she scrambled down the hall to Mr. Todson's office. "What did I do wrong now?" she wondered, afraid that one more mistake on her part would cost her the management position for which she'd worked so hard.

By the time Suzanne reached Mr. Todson's office, her pulse was racing and she was close to tears.

Stress-Filled Workdays

Suzanne's encounter with Mr. Todson was stressful before she even knew what he wanted. She reacted to Charleen's words ("he needs to see you now") as a student sent to the principal's office would—and Suzanne automatically assumed she was in trouble for doing something wrong.

Her emotional, physical and mental reactions put Suzanne's entire mind and body in a hyper-alert state. In her panic-filled mindset, how would Suzanne likely react to Mr. Todson if this is what he said to her?

"Suzanne, we need to quickly resolve a tricky situation with the Anderson account. Since you've done so much work with the Anderson file, I'm counting on you to solve this problem before noon today."

In this scenario, Suzanne requires every ounce of creative reserve in order to rise to Mr. Todson's challenge. Suzanne needs to come up with a creative solution—in a hurry! But Suzanne's anticipation of problems and troubles made her so upset that her creative thinking channels are gummed up with tension.

We've all had days like Suzanne's. Many jobs require split-second creative problem-solving, and in those instances, we can't afford to freeze up and be blocked by tension and stress.

An instant tension-reducing method Suzanne could have used is to block out fearful thoughts—a technique described in Chapter Five we call "thought stopping." You simply don't allow yourself to think anything scary, negative or bad. As Suzanne was walking to her boss's office, she could stop thoughts such as "I'm going to get fired, I just know it!"

To stop a troubling thought, scream "stop!" silently (in your mind) anytime a negative idea pops up. Next, think a pleasant, positive thought. This could be a picture (a tropical island, a garden, etc.) or words ("I am a good person," "I am safe and secure," "I can take good care of myself, no matter what," "I have always landed on my feet before, and I trust I always will," or "everything happens for the best").

By repeating this thought-stopping technique, you develop a positive habit of clearing your mind of needless negative fantasies. This frees your mind to focus on the tasks at hand. Thought stopping also gives you more energy as you remove the constricting weight of worry.

All Stress Is Rooted in Fear

Stress originates in fear. An external situation arises, and our fear-based thoughts in response to the situation create tension. We label that tension "stress." Here are common fears that lead to stress:

- "He doesn't respect me."
- "She doesn't like me."
- "I might be fired."
- "I'm incompetent."
- "I'm afraid of being poor."
- "He thinks I'm stupid."
- "I can never do anything right."
- "I don't know if I can do this."
- "He's going to leave me."
- "Others will laugh at me and think I'm a fool."

Traditional stress management courses focus on undoing the physical reactions to stress. They teach you to lie on the floor, put one finger over your right nostril and take a deep breath, then alternate with the left nostril. This method is impractical, however, because few people can or will lie on the floor and cover their nostrils at the office—especially in the midst of a crisis. Secondly, this method attacks the symptom of the stress (the physical tension), not its underlying cause (the tension-causing fears).

From Fear-Full to Fear-Less

Here is a proven method for melting your fears. I've taught this method to executives and employees of Fortune 500 corporations and other companies across the country. I continually get letters telling me how effective this seemingly simple method is.

When we become afraid, we are just like a young child afraid of the Boogie Man. How do you comfort a fearful child? By reassuring her that everything's safe and that she's all right. It might help to think of yourself as both the parent and the child—the rational part of you (the one that cares about your job) will be comforting the fearful part of you (the little child in you that is filled with fears).

1. First, you must remove yourself from the room where you first became afraid. You need to be alone with your "child" for a moment. This is important.

2. Tell whoever you are with, "Yes, I agree this is of utmost importance. I absolutely must excuse myself to go the restroom right now. Then I'll tackle this problem and help resolve it." No one will argue with you, or think you are weak, when you say you have to go to the bathroom.

3. Go in the bathroom stall, close the door and sit down. Take two extremely deep breaths. This will slow down your heart rate and help you get a clear mind. Only with a clear mind are we capable of creative problem solving!

4. Comfort your child. Tell her some loving thoughts to make her feel confident, strong and secure. The best way is to mentally state a few positive affirmations, such as:
   - "I am a competent, smart person."
   - "I am always able to resolve challenges and problems."
   - "I am cool and calm in a crisis."
   - "Challenges are my opportunity to grow stronger and learn new skills."
   - "I enjoy success."
   - "I expect to succeed."

5. Take another deep breath and hold on to your positive thoughts as you return to the "scene of the crisis." Don't allow your mental and physical state to return to a fear-full state. If during your problem-solving session you feel afraid again, combat that fear with an affirmation.

This method clears the cobwebs of paralyzing fears, allowing you a clear mind and access to your creativity. As Louise L. Hay writes in her bestselling book, *You Can Heal Your Life:*

"The only thing you ever have any control of is your current thought. Your old thoughts are gone; there is nothing you can do about them except live out the experiences they caused. Your future thoughts have not been formed, and you do not know what they will be. Your current thought, the one you are thinking right now, is totally under your control."

CHAPTER NINETEEN

Never Say Never: Success Stories of People Who Overcame Adversity

My favorite stories are nonfiction accounts of successful people who beat the odds. I love to hear about folks who kept going, refusing to give up on their dreams—and who realized those dreams.

Every successful person I've ever met has been through difficult times. I believe those struggles can either defeat you or make you stronger, depending on how you view them. Do you see problems as a challenge and a teacher, or do you see problems as a sign that you'd better give up?

Here are some of my favorite success stories. I've had the opportunity to meet and talk with many of these people, and I was both touched and impressed by their perseverance in the face of adversity. I find these stories extremely inspiring, and it's my pleasure to share them with you. If you have a favorite success story (your own, someone you know, or a famous person), please send it to me so we can share it with others in upcoming books.

Mary Higgins Clark

Mary was a widow and desperate for money to feed her five young children. Her meager salary from her secretarial job barely paid the bills, and her late husband's life insurance money was exhausted.

What could she do? She'd always dreamed of being a writer, and before her husband's death she'd even taken a stab at getting published. But forty rejection slips later, her dream had been stuffed away and forgotten.

But Mary decided to tackle her dream one more time, half driven by a need for the emotional outlet writing provided, and half by financial pressures. So Mary dragged herself out of bed every morning and wrote from 5:00 to 7:00 a.m., before the children woke up and it was time to go to work.

Finally, she'd completed a novel. Nervously, Mary mailed the manuscript out to several publishers and . . . she sold the book! Grann Publishers bought her first book for $3,000.

Today, Mary Higgins Clark is one of the highest-paid authors in history. Her record-breaking contract with Simon & Schuster guaranteed her a minimum of $10.1 million for four novels! Pretty good for someone whose confidence was pretty shaky as she was typing manuscript pages at the kitchen table, don't you think?

Joseph Weider

Joseph Weider is another publishing industry success story. He epitomizes the essence of a self-made person.

Joseph was a skinny boy at age thirteen, and the bullies in his Montreal neighborhood used to pummel him after school. Instead of shrinking away in fear, Joseph resolved to conquer the situation.

He'd read articles on body building and decided to pump up his own physique. But in 1935, barbells and dumbbells were hard to find. None of the Montreal merchants near Joseph's home sold weight-lifting equipment. So Weider made his own barbells from scraps at the local stockyard.

Joseph's weight-lifting regimen transformed his figure into a stockier build, which successfully deterred the bullies. Then he had an idea! There must be others like him, he thought—other people who wanted information about bodybuilding.

So Joseph started a fitness newsletter. He was seventeen years old and had seven dollars as his start-up capital. He also had a mother who discouraged his idea. She told Joseph, "You only have seven dollars to your name. You don't even own a typewriter. How are you going to compete with all these rich people in publishing?"

But Joseph didn't let his mother's negativity nor his lack of capital discourage him. With his seven dollars, he sent out seven hundred postcards soliciting subscriptions. He got enough prepaid subscription orders to pay for a rented mimeograph machine.

By his eighteenth birthday, Joseph had made a $10,000 profit! Today, Joseph is in his 70s and owns Weider Publications, which publishes such magazines as *Shape, Muscle & Fitness, Men's Fitness* and *Flex*. Revenues for the "skinny kid from Montreal's" business are more than $50 million a year and climbing!

Dan and Billy Baumgartner

How would you like to inherit a huge cattle ranch and oil field? That's exactly what happened to two happily married elementary school teachers named Dan and Billy Baumgartner. Little did they realize how much—and in what way—this inheritance would change their lives!

The Baumgartners had always struggled financially, since their meager teachers' salaries just barely covered the rent, utilities and groceries. Money just seemed to be out of reach for Dan and Billy. Other people were rich. Other people could buy whatever they wanted or go on exotic vacations. The Baumgartners thought they'd face financial squeezes for the rest of their lives.

Then they got their inheritance: a huge, rambling cattle ranch and an actively productive oil field. At first Dan and Billy were surprised and excited by their new property. They both continued to teach, and oversaw the management of the ranch and oil fields whenever they could.

But about two months after receiving this inheritance, they were in for another shock: property taxes were due on the cattle ranch. And the amount due was several thousand dollars! The Baumgartners had no idea how they could pay such a bill. They had no savings and hadn't received any payments for profits from the ranch or oil. If they didn't pay the property taxes, they would lose the ranch.

Many people would have given up in such a situation. They would have said, "What could I do? I couldn't afford it!" But Dan and Billy decided they had to make the money. They didn't even consider other options.

What happened next is amazing: Dan and Billy both quit their teaching jobs and got real estate licenses. They both knew exactly how much money they needed to make, and they were painfully aware of the deadline for paying the property taxes. So they did it. They persevered, without stopping, until they'd made enough in real estate commissions to pay the ranch property taxes. Then they kept making money. And more money.

Today the Baumgartners are financially secure beyond their wildest dreams. They continue to sell real estate, even when the economy is cloudy. The Baumgartners changed their financial status, but, more importantly, they changed their thinking. They discovered that life rises to your expectations. "If you want something badly enough, you will make it happen," is the motto they later summarized in their book, *The Beverly Hills Money Diet*.

Louise Hay

Louise Hay is another example of someone who discovered how our thoughts influence our lives and lifestyles. She has gone on to share her philosophy with millions through her best-selling books, such as *You Can Heal Your Life*.

When Louise was a young girl, she was raped by an alcoholic neighbor. Her family blamed her for the rape. Louise was also sexually and emotionally abused by her family. As a result, her self-image was pretty low. Louise believed that abuse was "normal," and that she somehow deserved to be abused. As an adult, Louise dated one abusive man after another.

Louise Hay describes in *You Can Heal Your Life* how her expectations and beliefs created the climate for abusive relationships in her life:

"The violence I experienced as a child, combined with the sense of worthlessness I developed along the way, attracted men into my life who mistreated me and often beat me. I could have spent the rest of my life berating men, and I probably would still be having the same experiences. Gradually, however, through positive work experiences, my self-esteem grew, and those kinds of men began to leave my life. They no longer fit my old pattern of unconsciously believing I deserved abuse. I do not condone their behavior, but if it were not "my pattern," they would not have been attracted to me. Now, a man who abuses women does not even know I exist. Our patterns no longer attract."

Today Louise Hay owns a successful publishing company, Hay House, with books distributed worldwide. She is a sought-after speaker and a woman very much in control of her life. The secret of her success? Accepting responsibility for her behavior and all the situations in her life. Instead of wasting time and energy blaming others for her misery, Louise Hay decided to make her life better. Using affirmations (see Chapters Five and Eighteen), she changed her expectations. As soon as Louise began to expect good things to happen, good things were then attracted to her. She says, "We are each 100 percent responsible for all our experiences." If you don't like your life circumstances, you must change your thinking.

"Deborah Ramsey"

Deborah Ramsey (the name has been changed to protect her privacy) is, at age 48, one of the most successful real estate agents in her state. At a time when most realtors sell an average of .9 (yes—less than one) houses a year, Deborah sells an average of 25 houses a year! Her story is especially remarkable, considering the disadvantages she had as a child and as an adult.

Deborah's mother married at a young age to escape an abusive household situation, and she was divorced after giving birth to two children. "We lived in poverty, and my mom remarried as a compromise to get money," Deborah remembers. "My mom was always unhappy in her second marriage, and she'd confide in me how much she wanted to leave my stepfather. But she couldn't afford to leave.

"I decided by the time I was in the sixth grade that I would never be financially dependent on a man like my mom. I started doing everything I could to make money: I baked cookies and sold them to neighbors. I picked beans and blackberries at farms."

All the while, Deborah's mother discouraged her from even trying to make something of her life. "She told me there was no need to go to college," Deborah recalls. "My mom thought I should set my goals on meeting a man with money."

To rise above her mother's low expectations, Deborah turned to self-help books and tapes. She devoured the positive messages like a starving woman, hungry for encouragement and inspiration. With these new positive expectations, Deborah envisioned a complete transformation in her life.

"I saw myself 'winning' and it happened!" Deborah enthusiastically explains. "The first thing I did was to write down all my long-term and short-term goals, spelling out exactly what I wanted to accomplish within ten years, five years, twelve months, one month and that day.

"Next, I reminded myself that no one was going to help me get started working toward my goals. I knew from the beginning I had to do it myself. Now that I was mentally prepared for action, I had to get physically in shape so I'd have the energy to work hard. So I prepaid a personal trainer to come to my house three times a week for the next several months, so I'd have no excuse not to exercise!

"I kept reviewing and visualizing my goals, and made my two-year goal within three months!"

Deborah's success story doesn't stop there, however. In 1981, after firmly establishing her real estate career, Deborah's life took a dramatic turn. "I found out I had breast cancer and at the same time, my doctor diagnosed me as an alcoholic. I had a double mastectomy, but the good thing about my cancer is that it made me quit drinking."

Deborah says she always looks for the positive in every situation. "I never allow myself to have a negative thought. If I'm down, I only give myself two hours of depression, then I say, 'Okay, that's enough depression,' and I force myself to think about something positive."

Perhaps the biggest and best part of Deborah's success story is that she has created the life of her dreams. She loves her work. She enjoys good health today and is a beautiful, vivacious woman. She is happily married to an attractive, loving and successful husband (who even cooks!). Deborah loves her life—she wouldn't settle for less!

Heide Miller

Heide Miller is another remarkable woman who showed great self-determination. At age twenty-five, she opened her first Heide's Frogen Yozurt (that really is how she spells it) store. The store was a success and she began to open others, until within a few short years, Heide owned one hundred-twenty yogurt stores in eight states.

Heide's upbringing prompted a lot of the attitudes behind her success. Her father has three doctorates and is a college professor of bioethics. Her mother is a homemaker. Growing up in the affluent suburbs of California's Marin County. Heide was painfully aware of how poor her family was. There were five children to feed in one of the most expensive areas in the country, and Heide's father's salary barely stretched to make ends meet.

"We never had enough money," she remembers. "It was very, very embarrassing for me, as a young girl in such a rich community, to be on food stamps. I saw that my mother was very dependent on my father for money. I told myself, 'I'll never be like that!' "

Heide says she always tried to do her very best at every endeavor, and she always followed her heart. That philosophy helped her win two U.S. World Games in gymnastics while she was still in high school. She went on to be a champion gymnast and body builder, featured in fitness magazines worldwide.

That champion spirit carried over into the business world, when she later started her Heide's Frogen Yozurt chain. "My father always taught me to work in careers I believed in. That's why he teaches bioethics, even though it doesn't pay a lot of money. It's what he believes in."

What advice would Heide give other women who long for self-employment? "Don't be afraid to fail," she maintains. "If you need to, get into therapy until you feel good about yourself.

"Behind every successful woman is a positive self-image," Heide says. "There's a lot of speed bumps on the road of life, but I never let them slow me down. Always remember that great spirits often encounter violent opposition from mediocre minds."

Erma Bombeck

Sometimes success occurs in small but powerful doses. Author Erma Bombeck shares an example of someone who was thrilled by a little taste of success. Though not technically a "success story," Bombeck's viewpoint about pursuing our dreams is very inspirational:

"When I slit open the envelope, a photocopy of a check for five dollars fell out. The note with it was simple and direct, 'I made this from my poem entitled *Youth*. Thanks for encouraging me.'

"Five bucks! What can you buy with five dollars these days! A pint of designer ice cream? One rose? A home furnishings magazine? A pair of pantyhose? Four gallons of gas?

"If you're Sarah, who lives in Louisiana, it can buy euphoria, with side orders of pride, hope and self-esteem and the discovery someone was willing to put a price on your talent.

"There's a lot of Sarahs out there . . . women who keep their dreams in a private little box hidden from the rest of the world. Occasionally, they take the lid off and look at it just to know it's still there and then get on with their business of living.

"It takes a lot of courage to show your dream to someone else. They might laugh. They might not understand. Worse, they might take it out of the box and drop it, and where would you get another one? Dreams are fragile, you know.

"Some people, in desperation, give up on dreams. They clean house one day and decide, 'This is ridiculous! I'm acting like a small child who refuses to give up a favorite toy.' So, they toss out the contents of the box—the short story, the idea for a business, the college degree, the job they would love to have, the child they want, the trip they would love to take.

"Then there are a few, like Sarah, who are willing to take a risk. They take the dream out of the box, put it on and start living it. They lay bare their ego to discover if they are equal to the dream or if they are equal only to the fantasy.

"I understand the fears and apprehensions of the closet dreamers, but oh how I admire the Mother Teresas, the Geraldine Ferraros, the Samantha Smiths, the Christa McAuliffes, the Helen Kellers and, yes, the Sarahs who write poetry on the kitchen table at night. Are they winners? Winning is not what they're all about. Neither are the rewards.

"What is special about them is they're dreamers who put it on the line. They had the courage to admit that what they wanted was just beyond their reach, but if they wanted it badly enough . . . anything was possible.

"They gambled. And for the risk, they were all rewarded with a legacy for others to follow. For some it was a trail that was blazed, an attitude that was changed, a place in history, a thought, a life that was touched.

"That's the difference between them and those who never take their dreams out of the box. They leave nothing."

These remarkable men and women inspire us because they did not let obstacles get in the way of their dreams and goals. They persevered, and they actually became stronger and more determined when challenges occurred. I love these stories because they remind me that extraordinary people are nothing more than ordinary folks with a mission and a vision who refused to give up. In that respect, every one of us who has weathered a storm—an abusive childhood, an unhappy marriage, the loss of a job, health problems, the death of a loved one or financial difficulties—and still had faith in a better tomorrow, is extraordinary.

Never say never!

A Letter to Readers

Dear Reader,

The Yo-Yo Relationship Syndrome begins when we allow others to shape our image of who we should be and how we should think, act or feel. We give away control, because we believe we'll get something valuable in exchange. "I'll be anything you want, if you promise never to leave me. Or fire me. Or criticize me."

This adult variation of our little-girl theme of "Please Daddy, I'll be a good girl, I promise!" is understandable. There's no need to criticize ourselves for this learned method of behavior. As little girls, we were taught that the way to get what we wanted was to look pretty and be "good." Translation: Be passive and the world will take care of your needs.

When we grew up and Prince Charming wasn't there to give us the castle and pretty clothes we had been led to expect, we felt betrayed. We blamed our husbands for not making enough money and blamed our parents for not sending us to medical or law school or for abusing us into victimhood.

No More Yo-Yo!

Instead of passively wishing someone would come along and grant us our fairy-tale wishes, taking charge ourselves involves three important decisions.

1. The decision to set about getting our emotional, physical and intellectual needs met on our own.
2. The decision to view these needs as non-optional. This means scheduling time for pure fun, physical fitness and goal-setting/goal-achieving.
3. The decision to choose fear-less thoughts, instead of fear-full thoughts. This de-stresses our lives and gives us access to our creative problem-solving abilities.

A Final Fun Thought

This book is the culmination of ten years of research and from giving workshops based on the material in this book to thousands of people. If I can leave you with one final thought, let it be this: I want to re-emphasize the importance of adding pure fun to your regular schedule.

Pure fun means something that gives you pleasure, with no other goals attached (such as scoring the most points or winning the game). Pure fun is childlike, silly, spontaneous and a great release from the mandatory activities of daily living.

I firmly believe that fun is a necessity, not a luxury. If we don't fulfill our minimum daily requirements for fun, we run up a fun deficit. We carry this deficit like a huge bag into our love relationships and into our work environments. This bag contaminates everything around it because it turns us into stressed-out, needy individuals. We unknowingly demand that other people take care of our basic psychological needs for love, appreciation and emotional intimacy. But the more we demand these essentials from other people, the further they run from us. And then our worst fears of abandonment all come true.

Other people can intuitively spot a fun-deficit bag from a million miles away—and they'll avoid it like the plague.

Keep your life healthy with regular doses of pure fun. If you view fun as a necessity instead of a luxury, there's no need to feel guilty for having fun, relaxation and pleasure.

 Always remember how good you felt when you saw your mother relaxed, happy and laughing. Contrast that to the scary feeling of seeing your mother tense or cross. Your loved ones feel the same way about you! They appreciate sharing laughter and fun with you.

When you relax and enjoy yourself, you give everyone a gift. You are not being selfish; you are being thoughtful and generous by sharing your good mood with everyone around you.

In the same way, your sunny disposition and relaxed state of mind will help you in business. Your coworkers, customers and employers will respond positively to your radiant attitude. You will have more energy to get jobs done in much less time. And your mind will be free to make creative solutions and inventions.

Not only will your personal and professional life improve as you add regular doses of Vitamin F (Fun!) to your daily life, but so will your mental and physical health. Research clearly shows that stress debilitates the body and spirit. A lot of solid evidence indicates that happy people have longer, healthier lives.

Every day, then, be sure to do at least one thing that's purely fun. Just as surely as you take a daily vitamin, do something just for the pure pleasure it gives you—every day. This is the Recommended Daily Allowance for Vitamin F. If you follow this prescription, you'll find everything coming up roses around you.

Here's one of the biggest bonuses from a daily dose of Vitamin F: You'll have so much more energy, it's as if you added an extra two to three hours to your day!

I wish you many fun-filled hours as you take charge of your exciting life. Please write and let me know how you've added fun into your life, and how it has affected you.

With Warm Wishes,

Doreen Virtue, Ph.D.
c/o Deaconess Press
2450 Riverside Avenue South
Minneapolis, MN 5545

READER SURVEY

My research is based on talking to women across the country and listening to their concerns, successes and difficulties. I don't believe in "arm-chair psychology," where a person philosophizes from the cushy comfort of her own experiences. I need to hear from you, in order to know what's important to you. Will you please take a few moments to complete the survey on the following page and drop it in the mail? Thanks for your help—and remember that by sharing, we all help one another.

Confidential Survey

Female _____   Male _____   Age____

1. What is your deepest personal concern? In other words, what do you worry or think about the most during each day?

_____

_____

_____

2. What do you think about the concept of "women's intuition"?

_____

_____

_____

3. Please describe a positive or negative experience you had with listening to your gut instinct, or by not listening to your gut instinct.

_____

_____

_____

4. To what do you attribute the successes in your life?

_____

_____

_____

5. What is your method for overcoming fear?

_____

_____

_____

6. What is your definition of success?

_____

_____

_____

Please send the completed survey to:

Doreen Virtue, Ph.D.
c/o Deaconess Press
2450 Riverside Avenue South
Minneapolis, MN 55454

Dr. Doreen Virtue is available for workshops and speaking engagements. For more information or to make arrangements, please contact Deaconess Press at 1-800-544-8207.

ABOUT THE AUTHOR

Doreen Virtue, Ph.D., is a psychotherapist and bestselling author who frequently appears on talk shows such as Oprah, Donahue, Geraldo, Sally Jesse Raphael and Sonja Live. She is a contributing editor of Complete Woman magazine and a regular contributor to *YM* and *New Body* magazines. Her work has been featured in many national and regional news outlets, including *USA Today, T.V. Guide, Woman's Day, Your Health, The New York Daily News, The New York Post*, an HBO special, and a *Prevention* magazine cassette series.

BIBLIOGRAPHY

Blomstrand, J., et. al. (1989), *Effect of Sustained Exercise on Plasma Amino Acid Concentrations and on 5-Hydroxytryptamine Metabolism in Six Different Brain Regions in the Rat.* Acta Physiologica Scandia, 136, 473-481.

Buss, D. M., *The Evolution of Desire: Strategies of Human Mating,* Basic Books, 1994.

Chaouloff, F., (1989), *Physical Exercise and Brain Monoamines: A Review.* Acta Physiologica Scandia, 137, 1-13.

Delaney, G., *Sexual Dreams: Why We Have Them and What They Mean,* Fawcett, 1994.

Delaney, G., *The Dream Companion: A Tool Kit For Dream Interpretation* (Audio Cassettes), 1-800-DREAMS1.

Folkins, C. H. and Sime, W. E. (1981), "Physical Fitness Training and Mental Health," *American Psychologist,* Vol. 36, 4, 373-389.

Frankl, V. E., *Man's Search For Meaning,* Beacon Press, 1962.

Hay, L. L., *You Can Heal Your Life,* Hay House, Third Edition, 1994.

Henriksen, S., et. al., (1974) "The Role of Serotonin in the

Regulation of a Phasic Event of Rapid Eye Movement Sleep: The Ponto-Geniculo-Occipital Wave." *Advances in Biochemical Psychopharmacology*, Vol. 11, 169.

Jeffers, S., *Feel The Fear and Do It Anyway*, Fawcett, 1990.

Jeffers, S., *Opening Our Hearts to Each Other* (Audio Cassette), Hay House, 1993.

Koella, W. P. (1988), *Serotonin and Sleep, in Neuronal Serotonin*, N. N. Osborne and M. Hamon, Eds., John Wiley & Sons, Ltd.

McCann, I. L. and Holmes, D. S. (1984), "Influence of Aerobic Exercise on Depression," *Journal of Personality and Social Psychology*, Vol. 46, 5, 1142- 1147.

Robbins, A., *Awaken the Giant Within*, Summit Books, 1991.

Schenkel, S., *Giving Away Success* (Revised Edition), Harper-Collins, 1992.

Schlessinger, L., *10 Stupid Things Women Do to Mess Up Their Lives*, Random House, 1994.

Sharpe, R. and Lewis, D., *The Success Factor*, Crown Publishers, Inc., 1977.

Smith, H. W., *The 10 Natural Laws of Successful Time and Life Management: Proven Strategies for Increased Productivity and Inner Peace*, Warner Books, 1994.

Tracy, B., *Maximum Achievement: The Proven System of Strategies and Skills That Will Unlock Your Hidden Powers to Succeed*, Simon & Schuster, 1993.

Tracy, B., *Peak Performance Women* (Cassette Series), Brian Tracy International.

SUBJECT INDEX

NAMES INDEX